SECRETS OF
THE UNIVERSE _____

This book is dedicated to all my students,
past, present, and future. ━━━━━━━━━━━━━━━━━━

SECRETS OF THE UNIVERSE

Discovering the Universal Laws of Science _____

_____ by PAUL FLEISHER

Illustrated by Patricia A. Keeler

ATHENEUM   1987   New York _____

ACKNOWLEDGMENTS

Thanks to my friend and colleague Donna Fout, and to David
E. Fisher, Professor of Geochemistry, University of Miami,
Florida, for reading my manuscript and for making valuable
suggestions.

Atheneum
Macmillan Publishing Company
866 Third Avenue, New York, NY 10022

Composition by Arcata Graphics/Kingsport, Kingsport, Tennessee
Printed and bound by Fairfield Graphics, Fairfield, Pennsylvania
Designed by Jean Krulis

10 9 8 7 6 5 4 3 2 1

Library of Congress Cataloging-in-Publication Data

Fleisher, Paul.
  Secrets of the universe.

  Bibliography; p. 208.
  Includes index.
  Summary: Examines the laws of physics that govern the
universe, covering such topics as planetary motion,
Newton's three laws of motion, gravity, the behavior of
gases, and quantum mechanics. Includes experiments
and activities.
  1. Physics—Juvenile literature. [1. Physics]
I. Keeler, Patricia, ill. II. Title.
QC25.F572 1987   530   86–14001
ISBN 0–689–31266–0

CONTENTS

1.

WHAT IS A NATURAL LAW?

Everyone knows what a law is. It's a rule that tells people what they must or must not do. Laws tell us that we must not drive faster than 55 miles per hour, that we must not take someone else's property, that we must pay taxes on our income each year.

Where do these laws come from? In the United States and other democracies, laws are created by elected representatives. These men and women discuss what ideas they think would be fair and useful. Then they vote to decide which ones will actually become law.

But there is another kind of law, a scientific law. You probably have heard about the "law of gravity," for example. Where did that law come from? Who made it, and what could we do if we decided to change it?

The law of gravity is a very different kind of law from a speed limit or a law that says you must pay your taxes. Speed limits are different in different places. On interstate highways drivers can travel 55 miles per hour. On crowded city streets they must drive more slowly. But gravity works exactly the same way no matter where you are. In the country or the city, in France, Brazil, or the United States, when you drop a ball, it will fall down. And it will always fall at the same rate.

Sometimes people break laws. When the speed limit signs

say 55, some people will drive 60 or even faster. But what happens when you try to break the law of gravity? You can't do it! If you drop a ball a thousand times here on Earth, it will fall down at the same rate of speed every time. It will never fall up or sideways or float in one place. You just can't break the law of gravity.

The law of gravity doesn't apply just to people, either. All objects obey this law: plants, animals, water, stones, and even entire planets and stars. And the law of gravity stays in effect whether people are watching or not.

The "law of gravity" is a *natural law,* or a rule of nature. Scientists and philosophers have been studying events in our world for a long time. They have made careful observations and done many experiments. And they have noticed that certain events happen over and over again in a regular, predictable way.

You have probably noticed some of the same things yourself. Gravity is a good example. When you let an object go, it will drop. Objects on Earth don't just float away. You know that from experience. Would you bet everything you own that a baseball tossed up in the air will fall back down again? It would be a safe bet. You'd be certain to win.

A *scientific law* is a statement that tells how things work in the universe. It describes the way things *are,* not the way we want them to be. That means that a scientific law is not something that can be changed whenever we choose. We can change speed limits or tax rates if we think they're too high or too low. But no matter how much we want to float instead of fall, the law of gravity remains in effect. We cannot change it; we can only describe what happens. A scientist's job is to describe the laws of nature as accurately and exactly as possible.

The laws that you will read about in this book are *universal laws.* That means they are true not only here on Earth, but elsewhere throughout the universe too. What is the universe? The universe includes everything that exists: our planet, our solar system, our galaxy, all the other billions of stars and galaxies, and all the empty space in between. Perhaps there are other universes elsewhere. But all we can ever know about is our universe. From all the evidence that scientists have gathered about the other planets and stars of our universe so far, it appears that the scientific laws that apply here on Earth also apply everywhere else.

In the history of science, a few laws have been found thanks to the brilliant discoveries of a single person. Newton's Law of Universal Gravitation and Einstein's discovery of relativity are good examples of this. But much more often scientific laws are discovered through the efforts of many scientists, each one building on what others have done earlier. Even when one particular scientist receives the credit for discovering a law, it's important to remember that many other people also contributed to that discovery.

Scientific laws *do* change on very rare occasions. They don't change because we tell the universe to behave differently. We can change scientific laws only if we have new information or more accurate observations. They change because scientists make new discoveries showing that the old law doesn't describe the universe as well as it should. Whenever scientists make a change in the laws of nature, the new law describes events more completely or more simply.

A good example of this is the laws that describe how the planets move around the sun. Astronomers once thought that the planets, sun, and moon all orbited the earth in perfect circles. But new discoveries and improved measurements of the planets' paths forced two great scientists, Copernicus and Kepler, to rewrite the laws that describe the motions of the planets. The sun doesn't revolve around the earth after all. The earth and the other planets revolve around the sun! Once scientists realized this, they had to rewrite the laws that described the motions of the planets, of course. You will read about those changes in Chapter 4.

Natural laws are often written in mathematical form. This lets scientists be more exact in their descriptions of how things work. For example, Newton's law of gravity, which we will learn more about in Chapter 6, is actually written like this:

$$F = \frac{g \times m(1) \times m(2)}{d^2}$$

Don't let the math fool you. It's still the same gravity you experience with every step. Writing it in this form lets scientists compute the actual gravitational force precisely in many different situations, here on Earth and elsewhere in our universe.

Physics is the study of matter and energy and how they behave. In the hundreds of years that physicists have been studying our universe, they have discovered many natural laws. Each of the chapters that follow will tell you about one or more of those great discoveries. Most chapters will also describe simple experiments you can do to see those laws in action. Read on, and share in the fascinating discoveries of the laws that reveal the secrets of the universe.

2.
ARCHIMEDES' PRINCIPLE

An oceangoing ship weighs hundreds or even thousands of tons. Yet it can float on water. How is that possible? The answer begins with one of the oldest and most famous stories in the history of science.

Let's imagine an experiment. You decide to take a bath, and so you turn on the water and fill the tub to the very top. Then, with the tub filled just to overflowing, you step in and sit down.

Even without trying, you know exactly what will happen. In fact, you'd better not try it, unless you want to do a lot of mopping up afterward! When you get into the tub, gallons of water will pour onto the floor.

According to an ancient story, this is just what happened to the Greek scientist Archimedes more than twenty-two hundred years ago. Archimedes sat down in an overly full bathtub, and water flooded over the sides. Seeing the water overflow gave Archimedes a brilliant idea. He was so excited about his new idea that he jumped out of the tub. Forgetting to put on his clothes, he ran through the streets shouting "Eureka!" which means *I found it!*

Archimedes had been thinking about why some things float while others sink. It couldn't be just a matter of weight. Greek ships were very heavy, and yet they floated. But even a tiny pebble sinks right to the bottom of the sea.

What Archimedes found in his bathtub was the law of buoyancy. This is now usually known as Archimedes' Principle in his honor. Archimedes' Principle says: Any floating object pushes aside, or *displaces,* an amount of water equal to its own weight. If a boat weighs 500 pounds, it must displace 500 pounds of water in order to float.

Imagine a boat pushing a "hole" into the water. If you measured the amount of water it would take to fill that hole, it would weigh just as much as the boat itself. A boat that weighs 100 tons must push aside 100 tons of water to float.

If you measure carefully, you will be able to see this law at work in the following demonstration.

Place an aluminum pie plate on a sensitive scale. Weigh it and record its weight. Now find an object that will float, like a block of wood, weigh it, and write down its weight.

Put the pie plate back on the scale. Place an empty can or wide-mouthed jar in the center of the plate. Carefully fill the jar with water to the very top. The water should be ready to overflow if you add just one more drop.

Now gently lower the block of wood into the can of water until it floats by itself. Some of the water in the can will overflow as the block pushes it out of the can. That's exactly what should happen.

After the wood is floating in the can, carefully lift the whole can, with the wood and water, out of the pie plate. Pick up the can very gently so that you don't spill any more water out of it.

Now weigh the pie plate with the overflow water in it. Subtract the weight of the pie plate itself. That will give you the weight of the water that the block of wood pushed out of the can.

$$\begin{array}{r} \text{Total weight of water and pan} \\ -\text{Weight of pan} \hphantom{xxxxxxxx} \\ \hline \text{Weight of water in pan} \hphantom{xxx} \end{array}$$

Compare the weight of the water in the pan to the weight

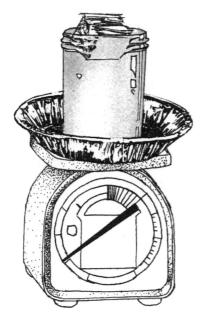

You can demonstrate Archimedes' Principle using a jar, a pie plate, and a small scale.

of the block of wood. They should be equal. The water that the floating object displaces weighs just as much as the object itself. That's Archimedes' Principle.

Archimedes' Principle is true for any object, in any situation. That's why it's considered a law. If an object can displace its own weight in water, it will float. If it's too heavy or dense to displace its own weight, it will sink.

Try the same experiment using a rock instead of a block of wood. The rock will sink to the bottom. As it does, it will push some of the water out of the jar and into the pie plate. Compare the weight of the rock with the weight of the water it displaced. You should discover that the rock weighs more than the water in the pan. The rock wasn't able to displace its own weight in water, and so it sank.

Archimedes' Principle can be described in another way: If an object is less dense than water, it will float. If it is denser than water, it will sink.

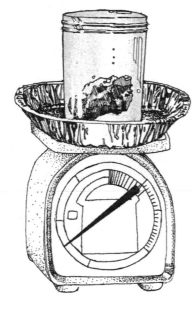

A rock doesn't displace enough water to be able to float.

Two different objects can be exactly the same size (or volume), but one can be much heavier than the other. A brick and a block of plastic foam may be exactly the same size. But when you compare their weights, the brick is much heavier. The brick has much greater *density*.

The density of an object is calculated by comparing its volume with its weight. The more mass (or material) that is packed into the same amount of space, the greater the density.

Imagine comparing the weight of our block of wood with the weight of a "chunk" of water that is exactly the same size and shape as the wood. If we could weigh the block of wood and the "block" of water, the water would weigh more. That means the wood is less dense than the water, and so it will float.

If we weighed a "chunk" of water the same size as our rock, we would get a different result. The rock would weigh more than the equal-sized amount of water. The rock is denser than the water, and so it sinks.

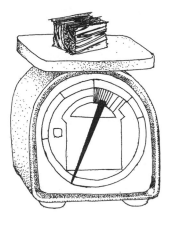 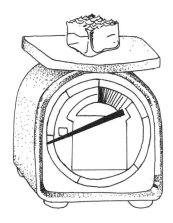

A wood-block-sized "chunk" of water weighs more than the block itself.

 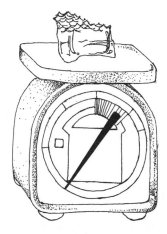

A rock-sized "chunk" of water weighs less than the rock itself.

The material an object is made of has a lot to do with whether or not it will float. But, as you might guess from the way boats are designed, so does an object's shape. Here's another experiment to show how true that is.

Tear off two equal-sized sheets of aluminum foil. Fold one into the shape of a canoe. Crush the other one into a small ball, squeezing it as tightly as you can.

Now place both pieces of foil in a container of water. The

The same amount of foil can be made into a floating canoe or a tight ball that will sink.

ball sinks right to the bottom. As long as it doesn't fill with water, the "canoe" should float. Because of its shape, the canoe can displace its own weight of water, and so it floats. The densely packed ball cannot displace enough water, and so it sinks.

A submarine is a very special kind of boat. It uses Archimedes' Principle very precisely to either sink or float. A submarine has several ballast tanks in its hull. When these tanks are filled with water, the submarine weighs more than the water it displaces. It sinks toward the bottom.

When the captain wants to float to the surface, he forces the water out of the tanks with compressed air. This makes the submarine lighter. It then displaces more than its own weight of water, and so it rises toward the surface.

To keep the submarine at one certain depth, the captain allows just enough water in the tanks to give the submarine *neutral buoyancy*. That means that the ship weighs exactly as much as the water it displaces. It stays just where it is, neither rising nor sinking.

Archimedes' Principle doesn't apply just to objects floating in water. It's true for any liquid or gas.

Helium is less dense than air. A helium-filled balloon will rise in the air because it displaces more than its own weight.

A balloon filled with the heavy gas xenon will quickly sink to the ground. It weighs much more than an equal volume of air. And a heavy bar of steel will float gently on the surface of a pool of mercury, an even denser liquid metal.

Archimedes made many other noteworthy contributions to science and technology. He invented a new type of water pump. He began the science of mechanics, the study of how objects move. He explained how to use levers to move heavy burdens. Although he hated war, he invented new weapons to help the Greeks defend themselves against their enemies. But the contribution for which he is best remembered still bears his name. Eureka!

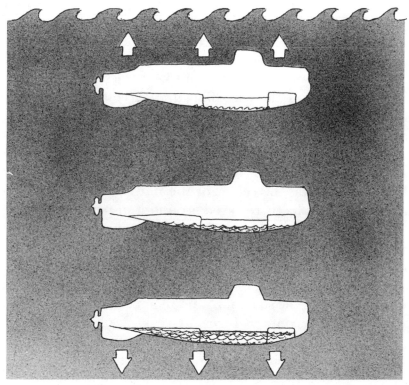

A submarine changes its buoyancy by adjusting the amount of water in its tanks.

3.

PLANETARY MOTION

Every morning the sun rises in the east. It travels across the sky in a great arched path. Every evening it sets in the west. The moon follows a similar path. So do the stars. It *looks* as though these objects must be traveling in great circles around the Earth.

People have watched the sky and kept track of the paths of the sun and moon and stars since the earliest times. And for thousands of years astronomers thought that all those heavenly lights circled around us while the Earth stood still. After all, we can *see* the stars moving in the sky. Standing here on Earth, *we* don't seem to be moving at all. Almost everyone agreed that the Earth was the center of the universe and that all the other heavenly objects revolved around it in perfect circles.

But there was a problem. A few objects in the sky didn't fit into the pattern. Sometimes these objects seemed to stop, move backward for a while, stop again, and then resume their paths across the sky. Because these heavenly objects didn't follow a regular path like the stars, sun, and moon did, they were called planets, which meant *wanderers* in Greek.

Astronomers plotted more and more complicated maps to keep track of the planets' strange wanderings. They drew maps with circles on circles on circles. But these complex arrangements still didn't solve the problem. The rules of science tell us that the simplest explanation is usually the best. It seemed very unlikely that the heavens worked in such a complicated pattern. Astronomers began to realize that the whole system didn't make sense. They needed a simpler explanation for the movements of the stars and planets.

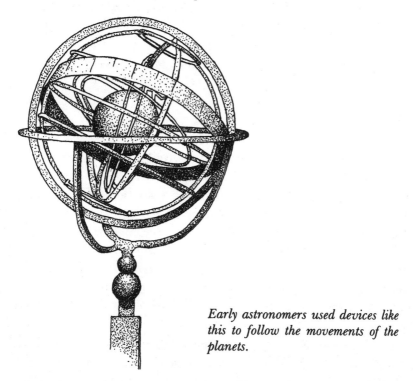

Early astronomers used devices like this to follow the movements of the planets.

At last, in 1543, the astronomer Nicholas Copernicus published a new explanation. Copernicus believed that the Earth was also a planet. He said that Earth and the other planets revolved in circles around the sun. Many people found this new idea very disturbing. Human beings thought of themselves as being at the center of the universe. But Copernicus' theory said that Earth was just one of several travelers around the sun. It made the Earth seem less special.

Another reason why many astronomers disagreed with Copernicus at first was that the Earth doesn't *seem* to move at all. It feels as if the Earth is standing perfectly still. However, others realized that everything on our planet moves right along with the planet itself.

The Italian scientist Galileo used a moving ship as an example. If a sailor at the top of a mast drops an object while the ship is moving smoothly, the object falls right to the base of the mast. The ship doesn't move out from under the object while it is falling. The sailor, the falling object, and the ship are all moving forward together at the same speed. Everything works just as if they were all standing still. Galileo argued that the same thing happens with the Earth as a whole. Everything is moving together at the same speed, and so we don't experience any motion at all.

After a while, most astronomers realized that Copernicus' idea was better than the old one. However, there was still a big problem. When astronomers tried to calculate the paths, or orbits, of the planets, their predictions still didn't come out right. The planets didn't follow the circular orbits exactly the way the astronomers thought they should. To improve their predictions, astronomers began adding circles on circles again. And once again their maps became much too complicated. There still had to be a simpler explanation for how the planets moved.

It was the Austrian astronomer Johannes Kepler who finally found the explanation in 1609. Kepler's discoveries are known as the laws of planetary motion.

Johannes Kepler loved geometry. He believed that the circle was the most perfect of all shapes. Because he believed that the universe was God's perfect creation, he thought the planets must travel in perfect circles around the sun. He was determined to prove that the planets traveled in circular orbits.

Kepler spent year after year making careful calculations of the orbits of the planets. He used the very best astronomical information available. The information had been gathered by his teacher and employer, Tycho Brahe. Brahe was the most accurate astronomical observer of his day. There were no better measurements than his.

For years Kepler tried to make Brahe's measurements fit into a pattern of circles. But no matter how hard he tried, he just couldn't make them fit.

Kepler finally realized that the planets didn't move in circles after all. They traveled in ellipses, or oval-shaped orbits. Kepler was terribly disappointed. But the more he studied his information, the more sure he was that it was true. In 1609 he published his First Law of Planetary Motion: Planets travel around the sun in elliptical orbits, with the sun at one focus of the ellipse.

Unfortunately, we can't do a simple experiment to show this law in action. Experimenting with planets would be rather difficult. But we can experiment with drawing ellipses.

An ellipse is like a circle that has been stretched out in one direction. A circle has one center point. An ellipse has two. Each of the two points is called a *focus* (plural: *foci,* pronounced "FO-si"). To draw an ellipse, you will need a pencil, six pushpins, a piece of white paper, a piece of cardboard, and a piece of string about 30 centimeters long.

Pin the four corners of the paper to the cardboard with four

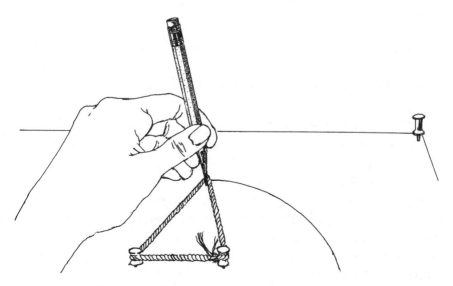

Use two pushpins and a string to draw an ellipse.

of the pins to hold it down. Push the other two pins in the center of the paper, about 5 centimeters apart. Tie the two ends of the string together to form a closed loop. Slip the loop over both pins and stretch it out as far as it will go with the pencil. Now draw with the pencil, keeping the string tight as you move it in an arc. Draw half of the ellipse this way. Then move the pencil and string to the other side of the pins and draw the other half of the ellipse.

Look at the ellipse you have just drawn. If it were the orbit of a planet, the outer oval shape would be the planet's path. The two center pinholes would be the foci. One of the two pinholes would be the location of the sun.

What happens when you change the distance between the two foci (the center pushpins)? How does the shape of the ellipse change when they are closer together or farther apart? Try moving the pins and drawing ellipses with several different distances between the foci.

The shape of an ellipse depends on the distance between the two foci.

You should discover that when the foci are farther apart, the ellipse becomes more "stretched out." When they are closer together, it looks more like a circle.

The foci of the planets' orbits are close together. So the orbits of the planets are almost circular, but not quite. It was the slight difference from a perfect circle that had given astronomers so much trouble. Once Kepler had discovered that the orbits were oval shaped, tracking the planets' movements became much simpler.

Because their orbits are elliptical, planets are closer to the sun at some times and farther away at others. Planets' speeds also vary as they orbit the sun. When they are closer to the sun in their orbit, they move faster. When they are farther away, they move more slowly. Kepler wondered if there was a law that would describe this difference in speed exactly.

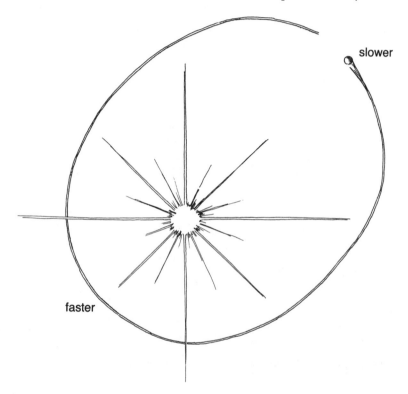

Planets move faster when they are closer to the sun and more slowly when they are farther away.

After more study and calculation, Kepler finally found it. It is known as the Second Law of Planetary Motion: A planet sweeps out sections of equal area in equal amounts of time as it travels along its orbit.

That may sound complicated. What does Kepler's second law mean? Suppose we mark the Earth's position in orbit on January 1 and again thirty days later on January 31. We could then draw straight lines from those positions to the sun, forming a pie-shaped wedge like this:

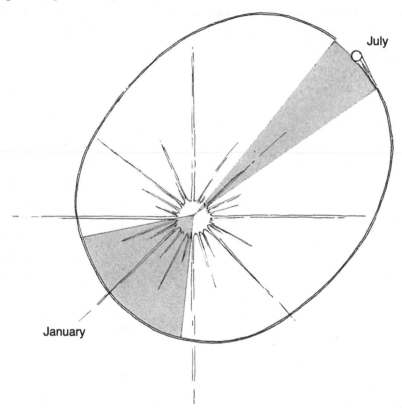

The two shaded sections have equal areas, even though the planet moves faster in January than it does in July.

That gives us an elliptical section of the Earth's orbit.

We could then mark another two positions, thirty days apart, on Earth's orbit. Let's say we mark July 1 to July 31. Again we can draw straight lines and form another wedge.

It happens that the Earth is closer to the sun during January than it is during July. The Earth also moves faster in its orbit during January than during July. So the two thirty-day wedges have different shapes. The July wedge is longer and narrower than the January wedge.

Kepler's Second Law of Planetary Motion tells us that although the wedges are different shapes, they have the same area. That means that they cover the same amount of space. Kepler's Second Law is a mathematical way of saying the closer a planet is to the sun, the faster it moves in its orbit.

Planets farther from the sun take longer to complete a single orbit than those closer to the center of our solar system. For example, Mercury revolves around the sun once every 88 Earth days. Earth itself, farther from the sun, takes 365 days to complete its revolution. Mars takes 687 days to circle the sun. And Saturn, the most distant planet known in Kepler's time, takes 10,752 days. Kepler guessed that there must be some law that would describe this situation too.

After much additional work, Kepler found his Third Law of Planetary Motion. The third law says: The square of the time of each planet's revolution is proportional to the cube of its average distance to the sun.

This is a mathematical way of saying that the farther away from the sun a planet is, the more slowly it travels in its orbit.

Here's a quick mathematical explanation of Kepler's Third Law: The *square* of a number is that number multiplied by itself. The *cube* of a number is that number multiplied by itself and by itself again.

Let's call the time of a planet's revolution around the sun *R*. Let's call its distance from the sun *D*. Kepler calculated the value of the fraction

$$\frac{R \times R}{D \times D \times D}$$

for each planet in the solar system. He discovered that the fraction he got for each of the planets was the same. The relationship between a planet's distance from the sun and the time it takes to revolve around the sun stays the same, whether the planet is close to the sun or very far away.

Why were Kepler's laws of planetary motion so important? First of all, they allowed astronomers to track and predict the motions of the planets more accurately. But the laws were even more important because they showed that planets follow regular, predictable patterns. That showed that it's not just objects here on Earth that follow natural laws. Other objects in the universe follow laws too. That was a new and very important idea. It let scientists expand their horizons tremendously. It told them that it was possible to study and understand the entire universe.

4.

PENDULUMS AND FALLING OBJECTS—GALILEO'S LAWS OF MOTION

Back and forth . . . back and forth. The chandelier in the great church swung at the end of a long chain. The young Italian scientist Galileo watched carefully. He sat very still and counted his pulse beats as the chandelier swung from one end of its arc to the other.

A pendulum is simply a weight swinging back and forth on the end of a rope or chain. The chandelier swinging from the cathedral ceiling formed a kind of pendulum.

Galileo used his pulse to time the swings of the chandelier. He had to use his pulse because in 1583 no one had yet invented an accurate mechanical clock. But Galileo was about to make the discovery that would make the invention of a clock possible.

Galileo noticed that it didn't matter whether the chandelier took a wide swing or a very short swing. It always took the same number of pulse beats to complete its swing and return to its starting point. Galileo wasn't satisfied with just this one observation, though. He needed more information before he could be certain about how pendulums behaved in general.

Galileo tested pendulums with different lengths, different weights at their ends, and different arcs of swing. The fact that Galileo used experiments was very unusual in the 1500s. Scientists, or *natural philosophers,* as they were known at that time, didn't use experiments to answer scientific questions. They used thought instead. If their idea seemed logical and sensible, they were satisfied that they had the correct answer. Galileo was the first great scientist to use experiments to test his ideas.

You can try some of the same kinds of experiments that Galileo did. All you will need is a sturdy string, several different fishing weights, and a watch.

Cut a piece of string a little bit longer than 2 meters (use a 7-foot length if you don't have a meter stick). Tie one end of the string to a support well above the ground. A plant hanger, a clothesline pole, or a standing lamp might make good supports for your pendulum. Tie a fishing weight to the other end of the string. Make sure it's free to swing without bumping into anything.

Make a chart like the one below. Measure the length of your pendulum and record the amount of weight you are using. Start with a small swing. Let the pendulum go, and carefully time exactly how long ten complete swings take. (One complete swing is the motion from the starting point of the swing to the other side of the swing and back again.) Then divide this total time by ten to figure out the time of a single swing. Don't forget to fill in your chart.

Length	Weight	Width of swing (L-M-S)	Total time (10 swings)	Time of 1 swing (Total/10)

Now use a medium-sized swing. Time ten swings of the pendulum again and record your results. Then try a large swing. After you have tried different-sized swings using the same weight and length, change weights. Tie a different weight to the end of your string and repeat your experiments.

Now shorten the length of your pendulum to 1 meter (about 3 feet), use the same set of weights, and repeat your timing measurements again. After you have finished timing those

You can do your own pendulum experiments using a piece of string and a fishing weight.

swings, shorten the pendulum one more time to about ½ meter (18 inches). Repeat your tests with the different weights and swings one more time.

Look at the chart. Notice the differences in the timing of the swings. Can you see what causes the difference in how quickly a pendulum swings back and forth? Are you surprised?

Galileo was. He discovered that the longer a pendulum is, the more slowly it swings back and forth. The amount of weight at the end of a pendulum doesn't affect how fast it swings. Neither does the width of the swing. The time it takes for a pendulum to swing depends only on its length.

This was a surprising discovery because it didn't seem to fit with common sense. Common sense would tell you that a smaller swing would take less time. And perhaps you would expect a heavier weight to swing more quickly. Galileo's experiment showed that, in this case, common sense was wrong.

After he completed his experiments, Galileo wrote a mathematical law to describe how to time a pendulum's swing based on its length. This law of pendulum motion soon turned out to be very useful. The Dutch astronomer Christiaan Huygens realized that if a pendulum of a certain length always swings at the same rate, it can be used to keep time. In 1673 he used Galileo's law to create the first accurate pendulum clock. From then on, scientists could make careful and accurate measurements of time in their experiments. And, of course, the new clock had many other valuable uses.

Now imagine the following experiment: You carry two cannonballs to the center of a high bridge. Both spheres are made of iron. Both are perfectly round. The only difference is that one cannonball weighs 1 kilogram and the other weighs 10 kilograms.

Now suppose that you drop both cannonballs from the bridge at exactly the same time. Which one will hit the water first? Will the heavier cannonball fall faster, or will the lighter one?

In the 1500s natural philosophers knew the answer to that question. It was obvious! Of course the heavier object would fall faster. They knew this to be true because the Greek philosopher Aristotle, considered to be the founder of the natural sciences, had written about these questions many centuries earlier. Aristotle said that heavier objects fall faster than lighter ones. After all, consider what happens when you drop a stone and a feather. In fact, Aristotle believed that if one object was two times heavier than another, it fell twice as fast.

For almost two thousand years Aristotle's explanation of what happens when objects fall was accepted as the truth. No one bothered to test it with an experiment. It just seemed sensible that heavier objects fall faster than lighter ones. But once again in 1634 Galileo showed that common sense isn't always correct.

If you did the experiment described above, the two cannonballs would hit the water at almost exactly the same moment! In fact, Galileo discovered that objects fall at almost exactly the same rate no matter what their weights are. The only exceptions to this law are objects that are affected by air resistance, like feathers or sheets of paper.

If you want to convince yourself that this is true, why not try it? Use two different-sized fishing weights. Drop the two weights from a high place at the same time. If you drop the weights onto a hard surface, you should be able to hear them land at almost exactly the same moment. Be careful not to damage anything or anyone when you drop the weights!

Galileo didn't have a good way to measure the speed and acceleration of falling objects. They moved too fast to be timed accurately with his water clock, which measured time by collecting a steady trickle of water in a container. He needed a way to "slow down" a falling object so that he could time and measure it. So Galileo decided to experiment by rolling brass balls down long wooden ramps. The ramps had polished grooves that held the balls in place. Galileo timed the balls as they rolled down the ramps. He understood that the balls were still "falling" to

If you drop them at the same time, different weights will fall at the same speed.

the ground. But they were moving slowly enough to let him measure how far they traveled during each unit of time.

The experiment showed something very interesting. The balls

seemed to accelerate (speed up) in a very regular way. A ball added the same amount of extra speed during each second. For example, if the ball traveled 1 meter during the first second, during the next second it would travel 3 meters. That means that after two seconds the ball would have traveled a total of 4 meters. During the third second the ball would travel 5 meters, and so at the end of three seconds, the total distance would be 9 meters.

See if you can figure out how far the ball would travel in the fourth second. What would its total distance be at the end of the fourth second? Write down the answer before you look at the next page.

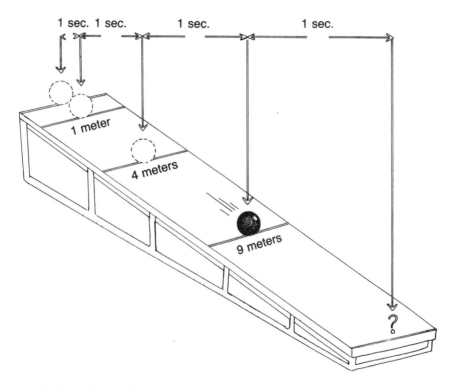

Galileo rolled balls down a ramp to study the acceleration of falling objects. How far will the ball travel in the fourth second?

During the fourth second the ball would travel 7 meters. And at the end of the fourth second, the ball would have traveled a total of 16 meters.

Incidentally, the metric system of measurement wasn't created until the late 1700s. Galileo couldn't have actually used meters or grams as his measuring units. He used other units that were common in his time.

Galileo tried his experiment with the wooden track held at a very shallow angle. Then he repeated his procedure using steeper angles. Naturally the balls accelerated faster on the steeper tracks. But one thing didn't change: The amount of acceleration was always constant. The balls always added the same amount of extra speed each second.

Galileo realized that if the ramp was lifted all the way up to vertical, the balls would *still* accelerate in a regular, uniform way. Of course, if the track were vertical, the balls would actually be falling freely. That was the evidence Galileo needed for his law of falling objects. Because the acceleration of falling objects stays constant, this law is usually called the Law of Uniform Acceleration.

The law says that falling objects accelerate at a uniform rate. As long as air resistance is excluded, the rate is the same no matter what the weight of the object.

Just how fast do objects fall here on Earth? Galileo didn't determine that in his experiments, but later scientists did. They found that falling objects accelerate at 9.8 meters per second (32 feet per second). That means that at the end of each second, an object is falling 9.8 meters per second *faster* than it did the second before.

Let's see what happens to an actual falling object. To make our calculations a little easier, let's round off the rate of acceleration from 9.8 meters per second to 10 meters per second.

Let's imagine dropping one of the cannonballs again, this time from a very high tower. An object that is dropped starts out with no velocity (movement in a specific direction) at all.

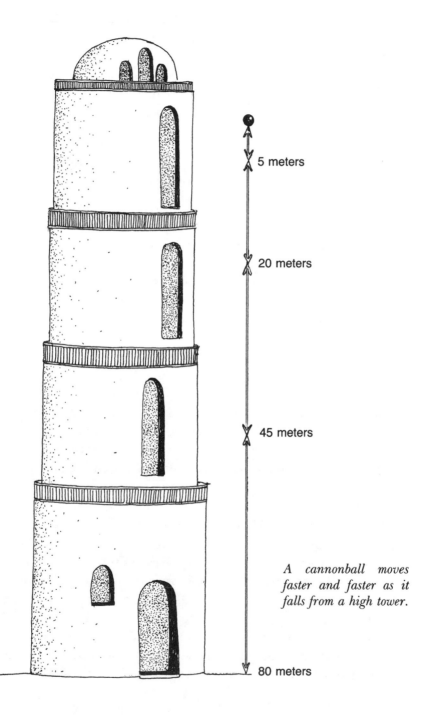

5 meters

20 meters

45 meters

A cannonball moves faster and faster as it falls from a high tower.

80 meters

When we first let go, the cannonball's velocity is 0. At the end of the first second, it has accelerated to a velocity of 10 meters per second. If we take an average of the velocities at the beginning and end of the first second, it's easy to see that during that second, the cannonball falls a total of 5 meters.

At the end of two seconds, the cannonball has accelerated to 20 meters per second. It has also fallen another 15 meters. Altogether it has now fallen a total of 20 meters in two seconds.

At the end of the third second, the cannonball is falling at 30 meters per second. It has fallen another 25 meters, for a total of 45 meters in three seconds.

At the end of the fourth second, our object is falling at 40 meters per second and has dropped another 35 meters. At the end of four seconds, it will have fallen a total of 80 meters.

As you can see, the cannonball is falling faster and faster each second. It will continue to accelerate until it hits the ground or until it is going so fast that the resistance of the air won't allow it to speed up any further.

Is Galileo's law true for every falling object? If you could take away air resistance, would a feather really fall just as fast as a heavy piece of metal? During Galileo's time scientists didn't know how to remove all the air from a container to create a vacuum. But a few years after his death, a method of creating a vacuum was developed. Scientists then conducted an experiment to see if Galileo was right. They placed a feather and a gold coin together in a vacuum chamber. When they were released from the top of the chamber, they fell to the bottom at the same rate. Galileo's law was proved true.

Galileo made another important discovery about falling objects. He realized that projectiles (like cannonballs or baseballs) also follow his law of falling objects. He discovered that the motions of objects moving through the air can be broken up into two parts. A projectile moves through the air sideways at a certain speed. But at the same time, it also falls down like any other falling object. And as time passes, its downward motion accelerates. If you shot a cannonball horizontally from

In an airless tube, a feather and a coin both fall at the same rate.

the same tower that we imagined dropping it from earlier, its path would look like the one below.

Of course, the cannonball would travel much farther sideways. But it would still fall to the ground at the same rate as any other object. If you dropped one cannonball and fired another

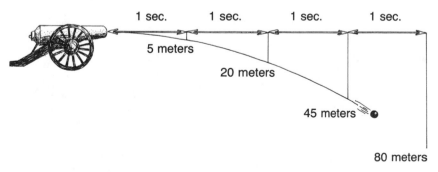

A cannonball follows Galileo's Law of Uniform Acceleration while traveling forward at the same time.

horizontally at the same time, they would both hit the ground at the same time!

Because he was the first scientist to prove his theories by actually doing experiments, Galileo is considered the founder of modern experimental science. But this great man did much more than study moving objects like pendulums and falling objects. He also used the first telescope to make many great astronomical discoveries. He found that the moon has features such as craters and "seas." He discovered that Jupiter is circled by moons of its own. He discovered that the Milky Way is made up of millions of stars. He was an important supporter of the theory that the Earth circles the sun and was even arrested and put on trial for that belief! For these and many other discoveries, historians consider Galileo one of the greatest scientists who ever lived.

5.

NEWTON'S THREE LAWS OF MOTION

It's a little after dawn on a warm Florida morning. On a huge concrete platform supported by a towering steel gantry, the Space Shuttle stands ready for takeoff. White plumes of vapor stream from vents in the smooth metal skin of the orbiter. Everything is quiet. Then suddenly a tremendous shower of flame erupts from the shuttle's engines. Gradually at first, then faster and faster, the gigantic but graceful craft roars into the sky.

The Space Shuttle is a miracle of twentieth-century technology. It is built with hundreds of special materials, wired with the latest electronic computers, and equipped with the most effective life-support systems the National Aeronautic and Space Administration (NASA) can devise. But the natural laws that explain how the shuttle takes off, moves through the Earth's atmosphere, and orbits the Earth were all discovered almost three hundred years ago. They were all discovered by the man who may have been *the* greatest scientist who ever lived, Isaac Newton.

When the Space Shuttle leaps into orbit, or when anything else in our universe moves, it moves according to the laws that Newton discovered and wrote down in the late 1600s. In this chapter we will look at Newton's laws of motion. In the next chapter we'll learn about his law of gravitation.

The universe is filled with moving objects. Wheels roll, birds and planes fly, trees sway in the breeze. Basketballs bounce, kites soar, boats sail, and people walk. Our Earth and the other planets in the solar system move. So do the moon, the sun, other stars, and even galaxies. What do all the various motions in the universe have in common? Are there any rules to describe how and why objects move?

The study of how things move is called *mechanics*. Archimedes studied the mechanics of simple machines like levers and wheels. Galileo studied mechanics when he experimented with falling objects. But it was the English scientist Isaac Newton who made the most complete discoveries about moving objects.

Think about what happens when a ball is rolled down a ramp onto a perfectly flat surface. It continues to roll, although after a while, it will slow to a stop. Early natural philosophers, followers of Aristotle, believed that the ball would need a continuous force pushing on it to keep it rolling. They thought that when the force was "used up," the ball would stop rolling.

Galileo realized that once a ball starts rolling, no more force is needed to keep it rolling. Galileo also realized that it is air resistance and friction (rubbing) against the surface on which the ball is rolling that finally make it stop.

What if there were no friction or air resistance, Newton asked? What if there were nothing to slow the ball down once it starts moving? Newton realized that unless some force acts to slow the ball down, it will continue on forever!

Now suppose we place our ball on a perfectly flat surface and steady it so that it is perfectly still. Unless we use some kind of force, like a push or a puff of air, the ball will *stay* perfectly still. It will never move by itself.

Newton understood that an object will change its motion only if it is acted upon by a force. Otherwise, its motion will be unchanged. If it is moving, it will continue to move in the same direction. And if it is standing still, it will remain still. That is Newton's First Law of Motion. It is usually stated as: An object in motion continues in motion and an object at rest remains at rest unless acted upon by a force.

This law is often called the law of inertia. *Inertia* is simply the scientific term for matter's property of continuing its motion (or lack of motion) until acted on by some force. This property of inertia is just what is described in Newton's First Law.

You can see Newton's First Law in action in the following demonstration: Get a drinking glass, a quarter, and a playing card. Place the card over the mouth of the glass and put the quarter in the middle of the card. Thanks to the law of inertia, it is possible to get the quarter into the glass without touching it. Simply flick the edge of the card with your fingernail. The card will go flying out, while the quarter will fall into the glass.

When you flick the card, the coin will fall into the glass.

The trick works because an object at rest (the coin) remains at rest unless acted on by a force. Your finger provides enough force to make the card move. But a playing card is slippery and doesn't create much friction against the coin as it is flicked away. That means there isn't enough force acting on the heavy coin to get it moving very fast. As a result, the coin falls into the glass as the card is removed.

The famous trick in which a tablecloth is pulled off a table, leaving all the dishes, silver, and glassware in place, works exactly the same way. When the magician snaps the tablecloth away, all the dishes are at rest. Because of Newton's First Law, they tend to remain at rest. The rapidly moving tablecloth doesn't produce enough force to move the dishes very much, and so they stay on the table. By the way, please don't try this trick at home. It takes lots of skill, heavy dishes, and a very slick tablecloth.

Inertia keeps the dishes on the table when the magician whisks the table-cloth away.

Objects moving in space have no air resistance or friction to slow them down. According to Newton's First Law, they should continue moving through space in a straight line forever. And that is exactly what happens. The *Voyager* satellites were launched into space in 1977. They carry messages of greeting from the people of our planet. Their rocket engines stopped burning long ago. But the *Voyagers* are still traveling through space, farther and farther from Earth. The *Voyagers* will continue on their journeys for millions of years, until something or someone stops them.

A space probe continues its flight long after its rockets have stopped firing.

Newton's Second Law of Motion tells us how an object's motion changes when a force acts on it. To explain it clearly, we need to define two terms:

Mass is the amount of matter or substance an object is made of. (Notice that it is not the same thing as weight. This difference will be explained in the next chapter.)

Acceleration is any change in the motion of an object. It can be a change in speed (either slower or faster) or a change in direction. As Newton's First Law tells us, an object can't accelerate unless force is applied to it.

Now let's consider a situation from everyday life. Suppose your family's car has run out of gas on a level road. Up ahead is a gas station. All you have to do is push your car there.

One thing that you certainly know is that the harder you push, the faster your car will roll. If only one passenger leans against the back of the car, the car may start rolling, but it will move very slowly. And that one person will have to work very hard. But if three or four people push, the car will move much more easily. Why? Because four people can provide much greater force than one can. The greater the force applied to an object, the more it will accelerate.

Would it make a difference if your car were a small, light-weight compact or a heavy luxury sedan? Which would be easier to push? The smaller car would move more easily, of course. The more mass an object has, the more force needed to make it accelerate. A large luxury car has much more mass than a little economy model, and so it takes more effort to overcome its inertia and get it moving.

The acceleration (or change in motion) of an object depends on two things: the mass of the object and the amount of force applied. The more force that is used, the greater the acceleration. The more mass to be moved, the less acceleration you will get with an equal amount of force. Those are the two ideas of Newton's Second Law of Motion.

The Second Law of Motion is often known as the law of acceleration. It is usually stated like this: The acceleration of an object is directly proportional to the force applied to the object and inversely proportional to the mass of the object.

Before we go on, it's important that you understand what *directly proportional* and *inversely proportional* mean. They are not as difficult as they might sound.

If two measurements are *directly* proportional, then when one increases, the other increases too. For example, if you are driving at 50 miles per hour, the distance you cover is directly proportional to the amount of time you drive. As time increases, so does distance. The longer you drive, the farther you go.

In the example of the stalled car, the greater the force used to push it, the more the car will accelerate. Acceleration is directly proportional to the amount of force being used.

If two measurements are *inversely* proportional, then as one increases, the other decreases. For example, if you are taking a trip of 100 miles, the time of the trip will be inversely proportional to the speed that you drive. The faster you drive, the shorter the time of the trip. As the speed increases, the time decreases.

In the example of the stalled car, the more massive the car is, the less it will accelerate when we push it. Acceleration is inversely proportional to the amount of mass being accelerated.

The law of acceleration can be written as a simple equation:

$$\text{acceleration} = \frac{\text{force}}{\text{mass}} \quad or \quad a = \frac{f}{m}$$

To calculate the acceleration of an object, we need to know the mass of the object and the amount of force applied to it. Notice that acceleration is written as a fraction. Force is the numerator and mass is the denominator. When we increase the amount of force (in our example, pushing with more people), the numerator of the fraction is larger. So the value of our fraction gets larger too. More force gives more acceleration.

If we increase the amount of mass (pushing a larger car, in our example), the denominator of the fraction gets larger. That means the value of the fraction gets *smaller*. So more mass will result in less acceleration, if the amount of force stays the same. That's why NASA is so careful about keeping everything in its spacecraft as light and small as possible. Larger, heavier spacecraft need more fuel and bigger engines to accelerate them into orbit.

If both sides of this equation are multiplied by m, this same law can be rewritten this way:

$$\text{force} = \text{mass} \times \text{acceleration} \quad or \quad f = m \times a$$

Newton's Second Law is most often written this way. It tells us that the force used to move an object (f) can be calculated by multiplying the mass of the object (m) times the amount of acceleration given to the object (a).

It also tells us that the faster an object is accelerated, or the larger it is, the more force it exerts. That should agree with your experiences in daily life. Think about playing a game of dodge ball. A ball thrown very hard will sting much more when it hits you than one that is tossed gently. The faster-moving ball has more force. A heavier ball will hurt more than a light one when it hits you they are if thrown with the same speed. The ball with more mass has more force.

We can see examples of the Second Law of Motion in action everywhere. When a batter swings and hits a baseball, the bat applies a force to the ball, changing its speed and direction. How far the ball goes depends on how much force is in the swing of the bat. Construction workers apply force as they move the steel girders they use to build skyscrapers and bridges. The more massive the girder, the more force needed to move it. The law explains why freight trains and jet airliners need such huge, powerful engines. It takes a tremendous amount of force to get all that mass moving!

Now let's look at Newton's Third Law of Motion. Picture a man paddling a canoe across a lake. Each time he takes a stroke with his paddle, he pushes some water toward the stern (rear) of the canoe. Each time he pushes this water *backward*, the canoe moves *forward*. Newton's Third Law of Motion is known as the law of action and reaction. It is usually stated like this: For every action, there is an equal, opposite reaction.

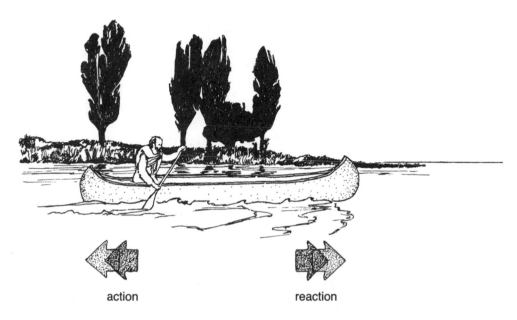

action   reaction

The canoeist's action *as he pushes the water backward with his paddle creates the* reaction *of the canoe's forward motion.*

As our canoeist paddles across the lake, he is pushing the water behind him with his paddle. That is the action. The reaction is the canoe moving forward in the water, with the same amount of force that the paddler used in his stroke.

Newton's Third Law describes why a rifle recoils, or "kicks," when it is fired. As the bullet fires forward out of the gun barrel (action), the force of the reaction pushes the gun backward against the marksman's shoulder.

Whenever you see a rocket or jet take off, you are seeing Newton's Third Law in action. When a rocket or jet engine is ignited, a tremendous amount of force is generated by the hot gases pouring out toward the rear of the vehicle. Newton's Third Law tells us that there must be an equal amount of force to balance this in the opposite direction. In this case, that reaction results in the forward motion of the aircraft or rocket.

Here's how to make a simple demonstration of the Third Law with a drinking straw, a balloon, some tape, and a ball of string. Tie one end of a long piece of string to something sturdy. Tie it well above ground level. A tree trunk, lamppost, or doorknob will work well. Slip the string through a plastic drinking straw, pull the string tight, and tie the other end to another sturdy object. The string should be tight enough so that it doesn't sag in the middle. Slide the straw to one end of the string. Now inflate the balloon and close off the end with a short piece of string tied in a bow. Securely tape the inflated balloon to the straw. Now untie the bow holding the air in the balloon and watch your rocket take off.

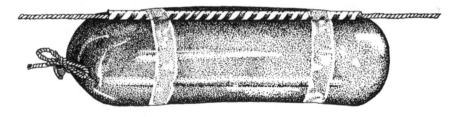

When you untie the bow, the balloon rocket will travel along the string.

Why does this work? The air escaping from the balloon exerts a force. That is the action from Newton's Third Law. The balloon "rocket" moves forward along the string in the opposite direction, as a reaction to that force.

Perhaps you've seen plastic toy rockets that are designed to be filled with water and then pumped up with air pressure. When they are released, the air pressure forces the water out the back of the rocket. The rocket leaps into the air as the water jets out the back. Of course, this toy works because of Newton's Third Law.

Can you figure out why this kind of water rocket goes much farther than an air-powered balloon rocket? It's because of Newton's Second Law. Water has much more mass than air. When the water accelerates out the back of the rocket, it creates much more force than the same amount of air would. The reaction to that force sends the water rocket soaring.

The Third Law is even at work when we walk down the street. Imagine what it would be like if, when we pushed against the Earth with our feet, nothing pushed back. With no resistance, we'd never get anywhere! Fortunately, when we push against the Earth with our feet, we do get resistance. Our muscles push against the Earth (action), and our bodies move forward (reaction).

Newton's three laws of motion were first published in 1687 in the book *Mathematical Principles of Natural Philosophy*. This book, usually known as the *Principia* (pronounced "prin-KIP-ē-uh"), is one of the most important and influential books ever written. Along with the laws of motion, it also describes the law of gravitation, which you will read about in the next chapter.

In addition to his discoveries about motion and gravitation, Newton also made important discoveries about light. He also invented a new kind of mathematics called calculus. Newton received many honors for his discoveries. The metric unit used to measure force, called the newton, is named in his honor.

Scientists and philosophers of his time were tremendously excited by Newton's laws. They began to think that the universe worked like a huge but predictable machine. Some scientists thought that if they could just measure all the forces and masses of objects moving through the universe, they could predict exactly what the results of any event would be. It wasn't until the twentieth century that Albert Einstein showed that even Newton's laws, as great as they were, couldn't describe *everything* that happens in our amazing universe.

6.

THE LAW OF UNIVERSAL GRAVITATION

Since the earliest times, people have known that objects that are dropped or thrown will fall back to Earth. The familiar saying, "What goes up must come down," is *not* the law of gravity. Isaac Newton's great discovery was that gravitation is a *universal* force. The force of gravity exists in every corner of the universe. It works the same way everywhere. Isaac Newton didn't discover gravity. He discovered that a single force is responsible for the motions of the planets, the moon, the sun, the tides, and falling objects on Earth. That is why his discovery is properly known as the Law of *Universal* Gravitation.

When he was a young man, Newton wondered why the moon endlessly circles the Earth. As he sat in his mother's orchard and watched an apple fall to the ground, he suddenly realized that the same force that caused this ordinary event must hold the moon in its orbit.

The Law of Universal Gravitation is stated this way: Any two objects attract each other with a force that is directly proportional to the product of their masses and inversely proportional to the square of the distance between their centers.

Let's take this statement one phrase at a time and see exactly what it means.

"Any two objects attract each other . . ." means that the Law of Universal Gravitation applies to *any* objects in the universe. It applies to apples, rocks, people, spacecraft, planets, and stars. Every object in the universe has gravitational attraction for all other objects.

But if that is true, why don't we see objects like apples or rocks pulling toward one another all the time? Because the force of gravity is a *very* weak force. It is so weak that we only notice it in very massive objects, like our Earth.

Even a huge object like a skyscraper doesn't exert enough gravitational force for us to feel. Compared to the pull of the Earth itself, its gravitational pull is unnoticeable. Although sensitive instruments can measure the gravitational pull of a giant office building, we can walk past it without feeling a thing. Even our own muscle power is strong enough to let us lift our bodies away from the gravitation of the huge Earth temporarily, whenever we walk, run, or jump.

Nevertheless, every object in the universe, from the largest galaxy to the smallest atom, exerts some gravitational force.

". . . with a force that is directly proportional to the product of their masses . . ." Remember what *directly proportional* means? As one measurement increases, the other increases as well. In the case of the Law of Universal Gravitation, when the masses of objects increase, the gravitational force between them increases too. Mass is the amount of matter objects are made of. To calculate the attraction between any two objects, the *product* of their masses must be calculated. That means that the two masses must be multiplied. Because of that, if one object is twice as large as another, it has twice as much gravitational force.

One of the things that made Newton's Law of Universal Gravitation such an important discovery was that it explained so many different things. One of the things it explained was Galileo's Law of Uniform Acceleration.

Think about the attraction between the Earth and a cannonball with a mass of 10 kilograms. If we double the amount of mass—to 20 kilograms—the Law of Universal Gravitation tells us that the attraction between the Earth and the cannonball will be twice as much. But if that is true, why doesn't the larger cannonball fall twice as fast as the smaller one? Remember, Galileo proved that objects on Earth all fall at the same rate.

The answer comes from Newton's Second Law of Motion. That law says that acceleration increases as the amount of force increases. But acceleration also decreases as the amount of mass increases. Gravity is pulling the larger cannonball with twice as much force. But the cannonball has twice as much mass to get moving too. The effects of the change in force and the change in mass cancel each other out. So both cannonballs fall at exactly the same rate!

Now let's look at the final part of the law: ". . . and inversely proportional to the square of the distance between their centers." Remember that when two measurements are inversely proportional, one amount decreases as the other amount increases. In the Law of Universal Gravitation, as the distance between two objects increases, the amount of gravitational force decreases.

However, gravitational force decreases by the *square* of the distance between the two objects. When you square a number, you multiply it by itself. The square of 2 is 2 × 2, or 4; the square of 3 is 3 × 3, or 9. The Law of Universal Gravitation says that if the distance between two objects is doubled, there will only be one-fourth as much gravitational attraction between them. If the distance is tripled, there is only one-ninth as much gravitational attraction.

This relationship is called an *inverse square* law. Gravitation is only one of many forces in nature that works according to an inverse square relationship. Other things that follow inverse square laws include light, magnetism, and electrical force. For readers who want to know more about the inverse square law, an explanation of why gravity and other forces follow this rule is given in the appendix at the back of this book.

Notice that the Law of Universal Gravitation measures gravitational force from the *centers* of objects. Newton found that the force of gravitation acts as if it is concentrated at the center of each object. Of course, the Earth's gravity doesn't come only

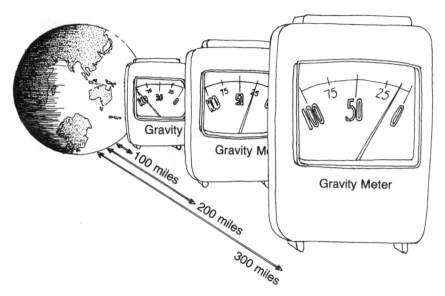

As you get farther from the Earth, its gravitational pull rapidly becomes weaker.

from its center. Earth's gravity comes from its entire mass. But gravity acts *as if* it comes from the center of the Earth. That's why objects fall "down" toward the center of the Earth whether they are in the United States, Australia, Japan, France, or the South Pole.

Mathematically, the Law of Universal Gravitation looks like this:

$$\text{Force of gravitation} = \text{Gravitational constant} \times \frac{\text{mass(1)} \times \text{mass(2)}}{\text{distance}^2}$$

or

$$F = G \times \frac{m(1) \times m(2)}{d^2}$$

In this equation *F* stands for gravitational force, *m(1)* and *m(2)* stand for the masses of the two objects attracting each other,

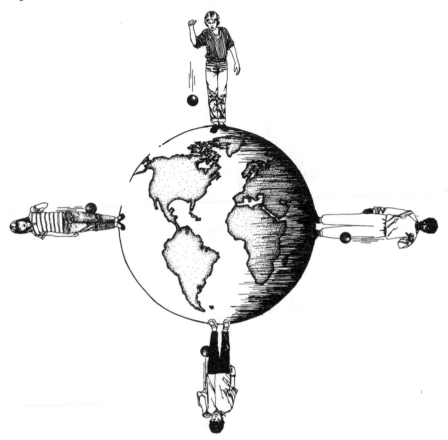

The center of the Earth is "down," no matter where you stand on our planet.

and *d* stands for the distance between them. *G* is a special, very small number called the *gravitational constant*. This constant allows scientists to calculate the exact force between any two objects.

Scientists in Newton's day didn't have equipment that could measure the precise value of *G*. But in 1798 the English scientist Henry Cavendish built a very sensitive device that could. Cavendish mounted two lead balls on either end of a long rod. The rod was hung on a very fine wire. Cavendish then moved two larger lead balls near the two balls on his instrument. The balls on the hanging rod were attracted to other balls by gravitation. That caused the rod and wire to twist slightly. Cavendish measured the amount of twist.

Since he already knew the mass of the lead balls, Cavendish could calculate the exact strength of the attraction that produced the twist in the wire. Then he calculated the gravitational constant, *G*.

Cavendish also used his experiment to compute the mass of the Earth for the first time. It turned out that the Earth has a mass of about 6 septillion (6,000,000,000,000,000,000,000,000) kilograms.

In the *Principia,* Newton explained how gravitation causes the moon to orbit around the Earth. Because of gravitation,

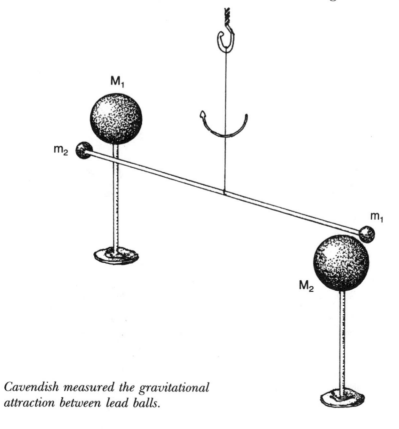

*Cavendish measured the gravitational
attraction between lead balls.*

the moon always falls toward the Earth. But the moon is also moving forward through space. The moon's inertia (Newton's First Law of Motion) keeps it moving away from the Earth in a straight line. So, as the moon falls toward the earth, it also travels far enough to move "past" it. The moon constantly "falling around" the Earth. This is called "free fall." Any spacecraft with enough speed can orbit the Earth in just the same way. The two forces—gravity and the motion of inertia—balance exactly, keeping the moon and Earth's artificial satellites in their regular orbits.

Newton's Law of Universal Gravitation also explained Kepler's laws of planetary motion. The planets "fall" around the sun just as the moon falls around the Earth. Newton's law says that the closer two objects are to each other, the stronger

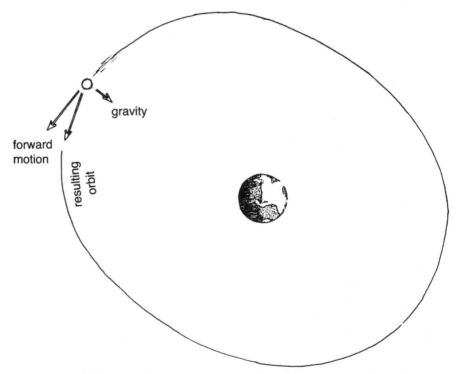

Our moon's orbit is a balance of gravitational attraction to Earth and the moon's own inertia (motion).

the gravitational attraction the two objects have for each other. So when a planet is in the part of its orbit closest to the sun, gravitation pulls more strongly on it, and it moves faster. In the farthest part of its orbit, the gravitational pull is weaker, and so it accelerates less. That is just what Kepler's Second Law of Planetary Motion describes.

Kepler also discovered that planets farther out in the solar system move more slowly (Kepler's Third Law of Planetary Motion). Newton's law also explains this. The farther away from the sun a planet is, the weaker the force of gravitation. Less gravitational force means less acceleration is needed to keep the planet in a regular orbit.

Newton also showed that ocean tides are caused by the gravitational pull of the moon and the sun. The Law of Universal Gravitation even helped astronomers discover new planets! The planet Uranus was discovered in 1781. But astronomers noticed that its orbit had a slight wobble. They realized that some undiscovered planet beyond it must be pulling Uranus with gravitational force.

Using Newton's law, two astronomers calculated where they thought the planet ought to be. In 1846 another astronomer pointed his telescope toward that spot in the sky. Sure enough, there was the planet Neptune. In 1930 the planet Pluto was discovered in a similar way.

Newton's description of the Law of Universal Gravitation also shows the difference between mass and weight. Mass is the amount of *matter* that makes up an object. Weight is a measure of the amount of *gravitational pull* on that mass.

As a simple example, imagine weighing yourself on Earth and on the moon. Of course, you will *weigh* much more under Earth's gravity than you will under the moon's gravity. If you weigh 100 pounds on Earth, you will only weigh about 18 pounds on the moon. That is because the Earth is much more massive than the moon. It has much more gravitational pull. However, your body will still have the same amount of *mass* in either place.

Although your mass *would be the same, your* weight *would be very different on Earth and the moon.*

When he wrote the *Principia*, Newton suggested an idea that was three hundred years ahead of its time. Newton had his readers imagine an extremely high mountain. The mountain would be so high that the top would be above the Earth's atmosphere. On the top of that mountain, Newton imagined a very powerful cannon. As the cannon was loaded with larger and larger charges of powder, its shots would travel farther and farther before they finally fell to Earth. If the force of the cannon were strong enough, Newton said, the cannonball would travel fast enough to fall completely around the Earth. Since there would be no air resistance to slow the cannonball as it fell, it would be launched into orbit!

Of course, in the 1600s there was no way this could be done. But three centuries later, we have rocket engines powerful

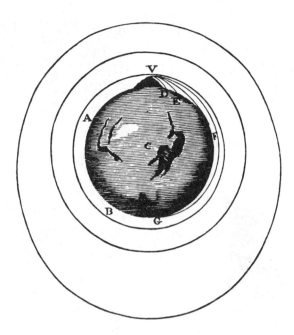

Newton's original drawing shows how it would be possible to place an artificial satellite into orbit around the Earth.

enough to launch a projectile through the atmosphere and around the Earth into orbit.

Now that you have learned about Newton's laws of motion and gravitation, let's look at a voyage of the Space Shuttle once more.

The Space Shuttle on its launch pad has a tremendous amount of mass. Since it is standing still, it has a tremendous amount of inertia to overcome in order to get moving. Remember that an object at rest continues at rest until acted upon by a force (Newton's First Law of Motion).

The force to overcome that inertia and blast the shuttle into orbit comes from the rocket engines. The blast of the engines forces hot gases backward out of the rocket. As a reaction to this thrust of gases, the rocket lifts off the pad and gradually picks up speed. For every action there is an equal, opposite reaction (Newton's Third Law of Motion).

With the rocket engines providing the force for the shuttle's acceleration, the spacecraft goes faster and faster. And as the rockets burn their fuel, the launch vehicle gets lighter and lighter, and the engines can accelerate it even faster. Remember that the acceleration of an object is inversely proportional to the mass of the object and directly proportional to the force applied to it (Newton's Second Law of Motion).

Finally, the shuttle is moving fast enough, at a distance far enough from the Earth, to put it into orbit. The Earth's gravity pulls the shuttle back toward the center of the Earth. But the shuttle has enough forward motion to "fall around" the Earth in continuous "free fall." Any two objects attract each other with a force that is directly proportional to the product of their masses and inversely proportional to the square of the distance between their centers (Newton's Law of Universal Gravitation).

It's amazing that Newton's discoveries still apply today, three hundred years after the *Principia* was first printed. It shows us how important Newton's laws are in our lives and how great an achievement his discoveries were. Very few human accomplishments last that long.

7.

CONSERVATION OF MOMENTUM

Picture two balls moving in the same direction at a speed of 1 meter per second. One is a 5-gram Ping-Pong ball and the other is a 5-kilogram bowling ball. They both have the same velocity. But can we say that they have the same amount of motion?

What would happen if both balls were to collide with something, like an array of bowling pins? The Ping-Pong ball would just bounce off the pins and fly off in a new direction. But the bowling ball would slam into the pins, knocking them down as it continued on its way. Even though the *velocities* of the two balls were the same, the bowling ball certainly would have much more *total motion*.

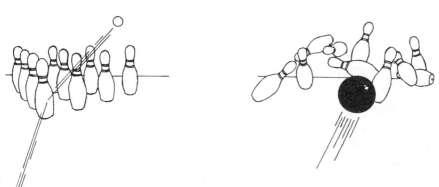

A Ping-Pong ball and a bowling ball traveling at the same speed will have very different effects on a set of bowling pins.

How can we measure exactly how much motion a moving object has? Knowing its velocity tells us its speed and direction. But we also need to know how large it is. We must know both its velocity and its mass.

The word for the total amount of motion of an object is *momentum*. Scientists actually recognize two different kinds of momentum. In the first part of this chapter, we'll look at *linear momentum*, or momentum in a straight line. Later in this chapter, you will read about a second kind of momentum, called *angular momentum*. That is the momentum of spinning objects.

Multiplying the mass of an object times its velocity gives us the total amount of linear momentum of an object. The mathematical equation for momentum is:

$$\text{momentum} = \text{mass} \times \text{velocity} \quad or \quad p = m \times v$$

In our example, the 5-gram Ping-Pong ball is moving at 1 meter per second. To calculate its momentum, we multiply the mass times the velocity. So the momentum of the Ping-Pong ball is 5 gram-meters per second.

Let's do the same with the 5-kilogram bowling ball. We multiply its mass times the velocity. Since 5 kilograms equals 5,000 grams, the momentum of the bowling ball is 5,000 gram-meters per second. Both balls are moving at the same velocity, but the bowling ball has 1,000 times more momentum.

Think about what happens in a collision between a moving vehicle and a stationary object like a brick wall. The larger a vehicle is, the more momentum it has. And the faster a vehicle is moving, the more momentum it has. That's why the amount of damage in a crash depends on both the size and the speed of the vehicle.

A large vehicle will do much more damage as it crashes into a wall than a smaller one. The larger vehicle has more mass and thus more momentum. Similarly, a faster-moving vehicle will do more damage than a slower one. The faster vehicle has more momentum because it has more velocity.

Newton's First Law of Motion says that the motion of an object remains unchanged unless the object is acted upon by a force. So the momentum of an object must also remain unchanged. When a quantity always remains unchanged, scientists say that it is *conserved*. Unless an outside force acts on it, the momentum of any object is conserved. The Dutch scientist Christiaan Huygens was the first of many scientists to recognize and study this law.

What happens when two or more objects are involved in an event? Is momentum still conserved? Let's consider a collision between two billiard balls as an example. One ball is rolling toward a second ball, which is standing still. The first ball has a certain amount of momentum, but the second has none. When they collide, the moving ball transfers some of its momentum to the stationary ball, and both balls roll off in different directions.

The momentum of the first ball is now divided between the two moving balls. Each of the balls is rolling more slowly than the one ball was moving before the collision. If you add the momentum of the two balls *after* the collision, the total will equal the momentum of the one moving ball *before* the collision. The total amount of motion is conserved. Huygens and others realized that momentum is always conserved in any object *or* any interacting *group* of objects.

The Law of Conservation of Momentum says that the total linear momentum of any object or system of objects remains constant, as long as no outside force acts upon the object or system. The objects in a system may move, collide, or fly apart, but their total momentum remains the same. The Law of Conservation of Momentum applies to any object in motion, from an atom to a galaxy.

The effects of this law can be difficult to see in the real world. When we experiment with real balls, some of their momentum is absorbed by the surface they roll on. We have to remember that the ball is only part of a larger group of objects, which includes the Earth itself. The momentum of an object that rolls to a stop or bangs into a wall doesn't disappear. It is just transferred to another part of the system of objects. When a ball loses speed to friction or collides with an object that is firmly attached to Earth, the Earth gains every bit of momentum that the ball loses. But the Earth is so massive that this tiny change in its momentum is completely unnoticeable.

For one more example of conservation of momentum, picture a loaded cannon mounted on wheels. The cannon is standing still. Its momentum is 0. Now imagine that we fire the cannon. The cannonball flies out the barrel of the cannon, and the cannon recoils, rolling backward with the same amount of force.

Newton's Third Law of Motion says that every action has an *equal, opposite* reaction. The cannonball and the cannon form a system of two objects moving in opposite directions with the same amount of force. If we add the momentum of the two objects together, the *total* amount of force in this system of

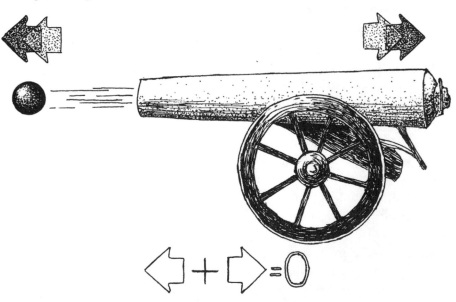

If you add the momentum of the cannonball and the momentum of the recoiling cannon, the total momentum is zero.

objects is still 0! In fact, Newton's Third Law is just another way of stating the Law of Conservation of Momentum.

We use our knowledge of momentum every day, without realizing it. Whenever we walk, run, or ride, we must constantly judge our own momentum to keep us from colliding into other people or objects. As you approach a stop sign on your bicycle, you must judge the momentum of the system of moving objects that includes both you and your moving bicycle. You apply pressure to the brakes according to that judgment. Fortunately, our brains have the ability to estimate our personal momentum very effectively, without a lot of mathematical calculation.

So far, we've looked at the momentum of objects in straight-line motion. But there is a second kind of momentum. Spin also gives an object a kind of momentum, which must be measured separately.

An object's rotation can be measured in revolutions per second. Picture our bowling ball and Ping-Pong ball again. Suppose they are both spinning at one revolution per second. Which ball would be easier to stop spinning? Obviously, the Ping-Pong ball could be stopped with much less force than the bowling ball. Even though they are both rotating at the same velocity, the bowling ball has a larger *amount* of spinning motion.

The amount of spinning motion that an object has is called *angular momentum.* It's called that because the spin of an object can be measured by measuring how quickly it rotates through the 360 degrees of a circle.

To measure angular momentum, we need to know how much mass an object has and how fast it is spinning. However, calculating the angular momentum of an object is trickier than measuring its linear momentum. That's because different points on a spinning object move at different speeds.

Picture a disk with a radius of 3 centimeters. That means it is 3 centimeters from the center of the disk to the outside edge. Let's put marks at the center of the disk, and at 1, 2, and 3 centimeters from the center. Our disk will now look like this:

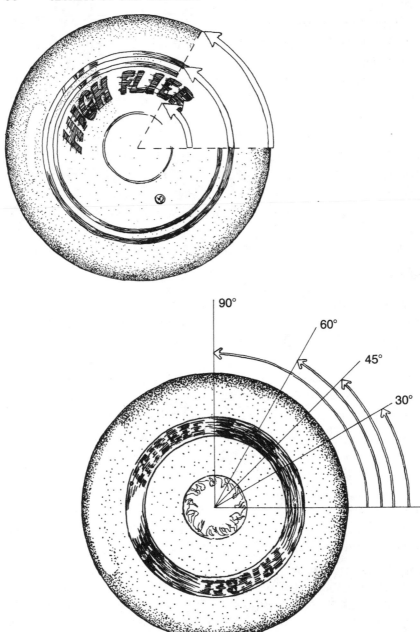

Momentum of spin is called angular momentum because the rotating object spins through a series of angles.

Now imagine that this disk is spinning at one revolution per second. Do each of the points we marked move the same distance in the same amount of time? Let's see.

In one second each point revolves once around the center of the disk. If we trace the paths of each point as it turns, we see that each point traces a circle as it moves.

You can see that the outer point of the disk travels much farther in one second than the inner points. The whole disk is spinning at one revolution per second, but different places on the disk are moving at different speeds! Since the outer part of the disk is moving faster, it must generate more momentum than the inner part of the disk. To compute the disk's momentum, we need to know more than just its mass and its rate of spin. We also need to know the distance from its center to its outer edge, or radius.

The angular momentum of a spinning object depends on three things: its mass, its rate of rotation, and its radius. Just as with linear momentum, the larger the mass or the faster the velocity, the more momentum a spinning object has. A spinning bowling ball has more angular momentum than a Ping-Pong ball spinning at the same rate. And a bowling ball spinning at two revolutions per second has twice as much momentum as the same ball spinning once per second.

But also, the farther the mass of a rotating object is from its center, the more angular momentum that object has. For example, our solar system is a rotating system of objects. It has an enormous amount of angular momentum, not just because the planets are so massive, but also because they are revolving so far from the center of spin.

The total amount of angular momentum of any object or group of objects is also conserved. The Law of Conservation of Momentum says that the total angular momentum of any spinning object or group of objects remains constant, as long as no outside force acts upon the object or system. Like conservation of linear momentum, this law applies to all objects, from atomic particles to spinning galaxies.

You can see conservation of angular momentum in the graceful spin of a figure skater. A skater starts a spin with his arms far away from his body. That puts his mass as far as possible from the center of spin. Once the skater is spinning, he pulls his arms close to his body. His mass is then much closer to the center of spin. His angular momentum *must* be conserved. Since his radius of spin is smaller, he must spin faster to keep the same amount of momentum. The next time you watch figure skating on television, you can actually see this happening.

You can experience conservation of momentum yourself with just a spinning stool and a couple of heavy books for extra mass. Sit on the stool and extend your arms, holding the books out from your body. Have someone give you a spin. After you are spinning, bring your arms in close to your chest. To conserve your angular momentum, you will spin faster as you reduce your radius by pulling your arms in.

Frisbees, tops, and toy gyroscopes also work because of angular momentum. When you throw a Frisbee or spin a top, you give the toy a lot of angular momentum. Its momentum can be changed only by an outside force, and the forces acting on

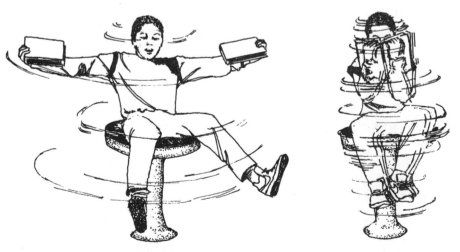

When you pull the books closer to your body, your rate of spin increases, but your angular momentum remains the same.

the toy are comparatively weak: air resistance and friction. So the angular momentum makes the toy very stable.

Precise gyroscopes are used as navigation equipment in ships and missiles. These gyroscopes are large masses spinning very rapidly inside movable frames. The spinning gyroscope is set in a specific direction, such as due north. Its angular momentum *keeps* it pointing north, no matter what direction the vehicle may take. The exact direction that the vehicle is traveling can be calculated by comparing it to the direction of the spinning gyroscope.

An object can have either angular momentum or linear momentum or both. For example, the Earth is both spinning and moving through space at the same time. A Frisbee spins and flies at the same time too. Both kinds of momentum are clearly very similar to each other. Each depends on the amount of mass and the velocity of the object.

We can even change one type of momentum into the other. For example, spinning lawn sprinklers change linear momentum to angular momentum. In a spinning sprinkler, each drop of water shoots out of the nozzle in a straight line—linear mo-

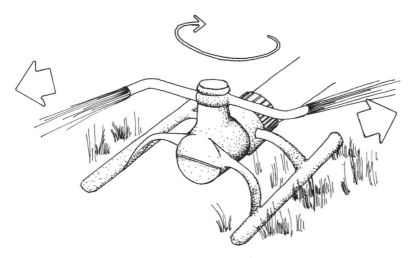

A garden sprinkler turns the linear motion of the spraying water into the rotating motion of the spinning sprinkler area.

mentum. But that action also causes the sprinkler to react by moving backward. That spins the sprinkler around, giving it angular momentum.

It's just as easy to change angular momentum into linear momentum. Imagine a spinning rubber ball. If you were to touch the ball with a pencil, the ball would spin against the pencil. The spinning motion of the ball would be converted to straight-line motion, and the ball would rapidly roll away. Angular momentum would have become linear momentum.

In every event, large or small, that takes place in our universe, the total amount of motion must always be conserved. That is the Law of Conservation of Momentum. So scientists know that whenever they observe and measure an event, all the momentum of the objects involved must be accounted for. If measurements show that some momentum seems to be missing, then researchers know that *they* have missed observing something and must look more carefully. Knowing this has led to several important discoveries, including the discovery of subatomic particles called neutrinos and the discoveries of planets, stars, and black holes.

The Law of Conservation of Momentum says that the momentum of any object or system of objects remains constant, as long as no outside force acts upon the object or system. If we consider the entire universe as a system of objects, then there are *no* outside forces. The universe includes everything there is. There is nothing "outside" it.

That means that the total amount of momentum in the universe must always remain constant. As galaxies collide, new stars form, and old stars explode, the total amount of motion in the universe will never change! Scientists believe that our universe was first created billions of years ago in a huge explosion they call the *Big Bang*. The same motion first created in the Big Bang is still with us today, spread among the vast number of stars and planets, atoms and atomic particles moving and spinning through the cosmos.

8.

OPTICS—THE LAWS OF LIGHT

When we look into the sky at night, we see the light from thousands of distant stars. We see the moon and the planets, shining with reflected sunlight. The whole universe sparkles with light. But what is light, and what natural laws describe its behavior?

The branch of physics that studies light is called *optics*. Some of the world's greatest scientists, including Newton, Huygens, Maxwell, and Einstein, have studied optics, trying to understand the laws of light.

One law that describes the behavior of light has been known for two thousand years. The Greek philosophers didn't know what light was, but they did know that it travels in straight lines. The Law of Reflection depends on this fact. When light bounces off a mirror or other surface, that is known as *reflection*. When you see yourself in a mirror, you are seeing light that has reflected from your face to the mirror and then back to your eyes. The Law of Reflection says: The angle of incidence is equal to the angle of reflection.

The *angle of incidence* is the angle of the light shining onto the reflector. The *angle of reflection* is the angle of the light bouncing off the reflector. The Law of Reflection says that those two angles are always equal. If a light shines on a mirror at a 45-degree angle, it will bounce off the mirror at that same angle. The same is true no matter at what angle the light is shining.

You can easily see the effects of this law by using a small mirror, a flashlight, some cardboard and tape, and a little bit of chalk dust or flour. Draw a straight line down the center of a square piece of cardboard. Then fold the cardboard in half along this line. Poke a small hole in a second piece of cardboard and cover the lens of the flashlight with it, taping it securely in place. That will give you a narrow beam of light when you turn the flashlight on.

Place the mirror on a table. Stand the folded piece of cardboard on the table, centered behind the mirror. This will give you a vertical line to use to compare the angles of the light

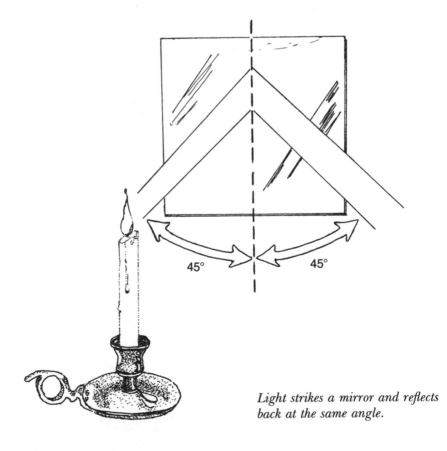

Light strikes a mirror and reflects back at the same angle.

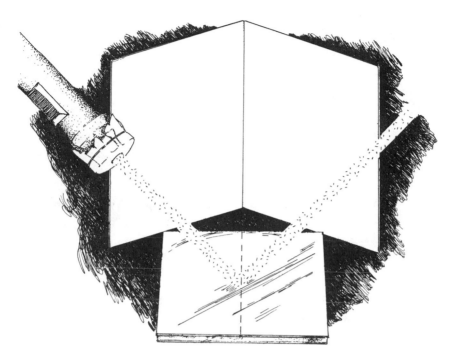

You can see the path of light reflections by shaking fine powder into the air.

beam. Shake a very small amount of the chalk dust or flour into the air, to make the beam of the flashlight visible. Darken the room and shine the light onto the center of the mirror.

Notice that the beam of light bounces off the mirror at the same angle that it hits the mirror. It doesn't matter at what angle you hold the flashlight beam. The angle of the light reflected from the mirror will always match it exactly.

Light travels in straight lines. But light also bends when it travels from one kind of transparent material to another. If you stick a pencil into a glass of water, the pencil will appear to bend where it enters the water.

Of course, the pencil doesn't actually bend. It *looks* bent because the light traveling through the water bends. This bending of light is called *refraction*. Notice that the pencil seems to bend

A pencil appears to bend when it is placed in water.

only at the surface of the water, where the water and air meet. Refraction takes place only at the boundary between two transparent materials.

Each transparent substance bends light at certain predictable angles. Refraction occurs because light travels at different speeds in different substances. The amount of refraction depends on the difference in the speeds of light in the two transparent materials. The bigger the difference in light speed between the two materials, the more the light will be bent as it passes between them.

Light travels faster in air than it does in water. When light moves from air to water, it slows down. And as it does, it also refracts, or bends. Light travels even more slowly in glass. When light moves from air to glass, it bends even more. A pencil placed partly behind a thick piece of glass would seem to bend more than the pencil in water.

One scientist who studied optics was Isaac Newton. Newton knew that when sunlight is refracted in a glass prism, the white light breaks up into a rainbow of colors, called a *spectrum*. Newton proved that sunlight is actually composed of all the colors of the rainbow.

Many years later the astronomer William Herschel discovered the existence of another kind of light, light that can't be seen. In 1800 Herschel was measuring the temperature of the different colors in the spectrum. He wanted to find out whether red, orange, yellow, green, or blue light produced the most heat. He used a glass prism to break sunlight into a spectrum. Then he measured the temperature of each of the colors with a thermometer.

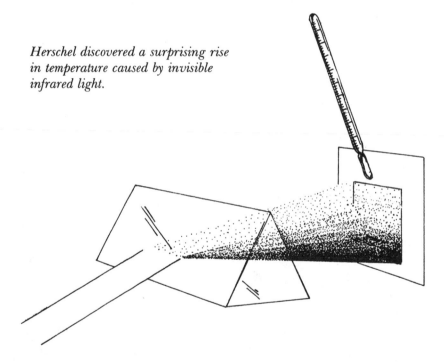

Herschel discovered a surprising rise in temperature caused by invisible infrared light.

Herschel found that the hottest part of the spectrum was alongside the red part, in a place where he couldn't see any light at all! But the thermometer proved that some invisible light rays were there. Herschel had discovered the existence of *infrared light.*

One year later light on the other side of the visible spectrum was found. This light couldn't be seen either, but it did form images on photographic plates. This light became known as *ultraviolet light.* In the mid-1800s James Clerk Maxwell showed that the spectrum of light includes much more than just the light we can see. We now know that the entire spectrum includes not just visible light, but radio waves, infrared light, ultraviolet light, X-rays, and gamma rays.

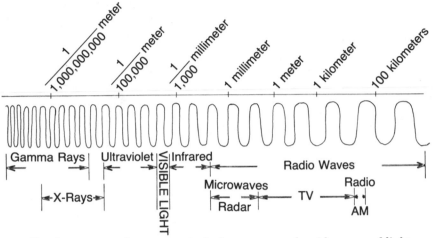

The electromagnetic spectrum includes an extremely wide range of light waves.

Newton's studies of light started one of the longest debates in the history of science. The debate, which wasn't settled for more than two hundred years, was over the question of whether light is a shower of tiny particles or a series of waves.

To understand the question, you need to know something about the behavior of waves. Waves can be seen most easily in a wave tank. To make a wave tank at home, you'll need a clear glass baking dish, a sheet of white paper, and a bright desk lamp. You will also need two pencils and several small blocks of wood to make obstacles for the waves.

Fill the baking dish about two-thirds full of water. Place it on a table, on top of the sheet of paper. Place the lamp so that it shines down on the water from directly above. Now tap the water in the pan with the eraser end of a pencil to create some waves. You'll see that the waves create shadows on the paper below, making them easier to see. Remember that the waves you are seeing are *water* waves, but other waves, including light, have similar properties.

Now place a small wooden block in the pan as an obstacle. Make some waves with your pencil on one side of the block. Watch what happens when the waves go past the obstacle.

Notice that the waves curve around the obstacle and travel into the part of the tank that is blocked off. This curving of waves around an obstacle is called *diffraction*. Diffraction is a characteristic of all waves.

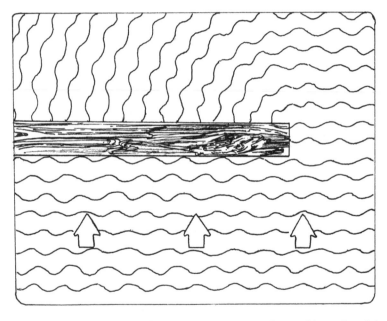

In a wave tank waves diffract, or curve, around an object placed in their path.

To scientists in the 1600s, light didn't seem to diffract the way other waves do. Light seems to travel in straight lines, instead of curving around obstacles. If you place an object in the sun, it casts a shadow. If light diffracted as water waves do, you would expect the light to bend around the object and make a fuzzy shadow. But light casts a shadow with sharp edges.

Because of this, Newton believed that light must be made of many tiny, swift particles moving in straight paths. When an object interrupts the particles, sharp-edged shadows are the result.

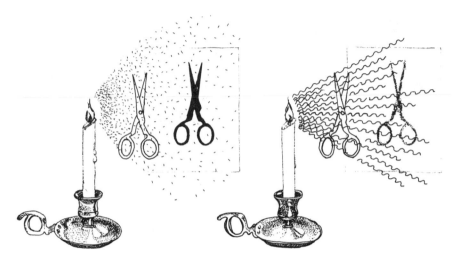

If light were made of particles, you would expect sharp shadows (left). *If light were made of waves, you would expect the shadow to be less distinct* (right).

After Newton suggested that light is made of particles, two other noted scientists disagreed. Robert Hooke and Christiaan Huygens pointed out that light also behaves like waves. Let's use the wave tank again to show their side of the argument.

In your wave tank, block off one section, leaving only a small central opening to the rest of the tank (see diagram next page). With your pencil, make some waves in the blocked section of the tank. Notice what happens when they pass through the opening.

The waves coming through the opening spread out just the way they spread out from the source of the waves itself. Huygens noted that any point along a wave can act as if it is a new *source* of more waves. The waves from this new source will

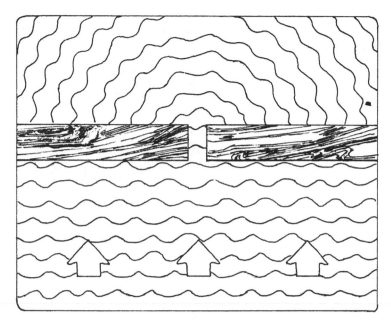

In a wave tank waves passing through a small opening spread out just as if the opening were the actual source of the waves.

have the same characteristics as the original waves. This rule is known as Huygens' Principle.

That's just what happens when you allow light to shine through a small hole. It spreads out from the opening just as if that opening were the source of the light.

Huygens also pointed out that if light were made of waves, that would explain its property of refraction. Light waves moving through different materials would travel at different speeds. The change of speed would cause the waves to bend. It was harder to explain why "particles" of light should bend as they pass into water or glass.

Waves have another interesting behavior, which is called *interference*. To see interference in your wave tank, you will need to make waves with two pencils. Hold the pencils a couple of inches apart. Then tap the surface of the water with both of

Light passing through a small opening behaves as if the opening itself were the light source.

them at the same time, in a regular pattern, creating two sets of waves.

Notice that as the two sets of waves overlap and cross, they interact with each other. In some places they cancel each other out, and in other places they add to each other's effects. This is called interference. If you keep up a steady pattern of waves with regular movements of your pencils, you should get a steady pattern of interference.

It's a characteristic of waves that they produce interference

*Two wave sources in a wave tank
produce a pattern of interference.*

patterns as they cross each other. When streams of *particles* cross, we would expect them to collide. No one has observed collisions when two beams of light shine across each other. But does light produce interference?

In 1801 the English physicist Thomas Young proved that light does diffract and does produce interference patterns, just as other waves do. It seemed that the light/particle question was finally resolved.

You can easily see an interference pattern of light using two pencils and your desk lamp. Hold the two pencils in front of your eye as you look toward the lamp. Move the pencils closer together, until they are almost touching. You will see a pattern of very fine light and dark lines. That is the interference pattern produced as light from the lamp passes through the narrow

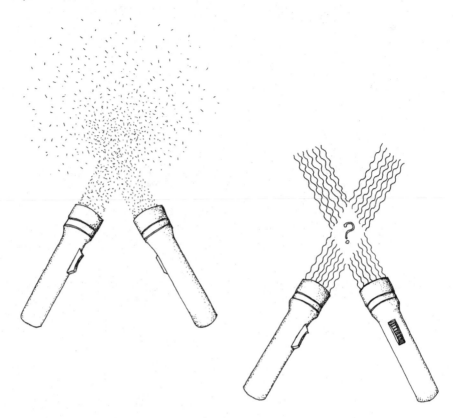

What happens when two beams of light intersect? Do they collide like particles or create interference like waves?

slit between the two pencils. The dark lines are the places where the waves of light are canceling each other out. Since light produces interference patterns as other waves do, it too must be a wave.

Young also calculated the actual size of light waves. The wavelengths of light waves are *very* small, but Young managed to measure them. Different colors of light turned out to have different wavelengths. Young found that the wavelength of red light is about 76 millionths of a centimeter. The wavelength of blue light is even smaller, about 38 millionths of a centimeter.

Young's measurements explained why the diffraction of light

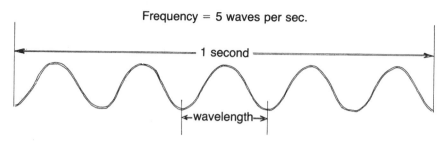

Waves can be measured by their wavelength or by their frequency.

is so hard to see. Diffraction occurs when waves bend around an obstacle. But light waves are so tiny that they can bend only around tiny obstacles, obstacles not much bigger than the size of atoms.

By the mid-1800s it seemed certain that light was made of waves. But even then the question wasn't settled. Around 1900 new discoveries by Max Planck and Albert Einstein brought back the particle theory again. The end result turned out to be that both sides of the debate were right! Light usually behaves like a wave, but it acts like a particle too.

Is there a law which describes the brightness of light? Yes. The faint stars that we see in the night sky are actually blazing suns. Their light is much dimmer after its long journey to our planet. The farther you get from a light source, the less bright the light appears. In fact, the intensity of light from any source decreases very rapidly as the distance from the source increases. The decrease is proportional to the *square* of the distance. Squaring the distance means multiplying the distance times itself.

This special relationship between brightness and the distance from the light source is called an *inverse square* relationship. Many other forces in nature weaken with distance in similar ways. A more detailed explanation of why this is so is given in the appendix at the back of this book. In the meantime, just think how much light our sun must produce. It is extremely bright, even though we are about 93 million miles away!

We need to consider one more fact about light—its speed. Galileo was the first scientist to try measuring the speed of light. He stood on a hill with a covered lantern and placed an assistant on a distant hill with a second lantern. He uncovered his lantern. As soon as his assistant saw the light, he was supposed to uncover his lantern. Galileo planned to measure the time it took for him to receive the signal back again.

Unfortunately, the experiment didn't work. The light seemed to travel between the two hilltops almost instantaneously. Light moves so fast that measuring its speed is very difficult.

The first successful attempt to measure the speed of light used the Earth's orbit as a measuring stick. The Danish astronomer Olaus Roemer knew when eclipses of Jupiter's moons were scheduled to occur in the late 1600s. He noticed that the timing of the eclipses varied, depending on where Jupiter and Earth were in their orbits. If the two planets were on opposite sides of the sun, the eclipses were a few minutes late. If the two planets were on the same side of the sun, the eclipses were a few minutes early.

Roemer realized that the *time* difference was caused by the difference in *distance* that the light from Jupiter's moon had to travel before it was seen on Earth. Roemer knew the approximate diameter of Earth's orbit. He knew how much extra distance the light had to travel to cross that orbit. So he could estimate how fast the light traveled to cross that distance. Roemer calculated that light travels at about 150,000 miles per second.

In 1849 the French physicist Armand Fizeau was the first scientist to create a device to measure the speed of light in a laboratory experiment. Since that time many other researchers have made more and more exact measurements of the speed of light. The most famous of them was the American physicist Albert Michelson. He devoted most of his life to determining the speed of light accurately. Michelson won the Nobel Prize

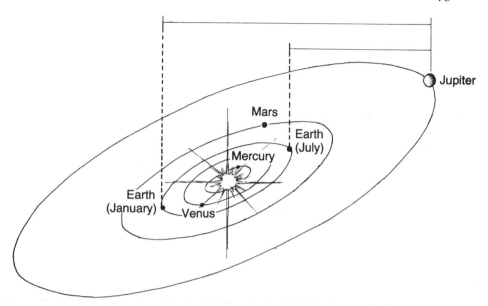

Roemer used different positions of the Earth's orbit to measure the speed of the sunlight reflected from Jupiter.

in 1907, in honor of the many ingenious experiments he used to measure the speed of light as precisely as possible.

Scientists now put the speed of light at 186,281.7 miles per second, or 299,792.8 kilometers per second. Those speeds are usually rounded off to 186,000 miles per second, or 300,000 kilometers per second. As you will see in Chapter 19, this is a very important measurement. The speed of light can be considered the "speed limit" of the universe. As far as we know, it is impossible for anything to travel faster than the speed of light.

The speed of light is 300,000 kilometers per second *in a vacuum* (totally empty space). Light travels almost as fast in air. In other materials, such as water or glass, the speed of light is much slower. For example, light travels about 225,000 kilometers per second in water and about 200,000 per second in glass. It is this difference in speed that causes light to refract, or bend, when it moves between one substance and another.

Light is such a familiar part of our everyday world that it's easy to forget how special and important it is. We can see our world only because it is bathed in a constant stream of light, which reflects from the objects around us and into our eyes. The universe is full of light traveling at enormous speeds from distant stars and galaxies. It is this light that lets us know what's "out there" beyond our own world. Light is our most important connection to everything in the universe that lies beyond our own planet. Without an understanding of light, science could never understand the rest of the universe at all.

9.

THE LAW OF CONSERVATION OF MATTER

Magicians love to make objects appear and disappear. Coins suddenly appear behind someone's ear, a rabbit pops out of an empty hat, or a beautiful lady vanishes into thin air. Almost every magician depends on mysterious appearances and disappearances for many of his tricks.

When we see a magician make something appear or disappear, we're fascinated. Why? We're amazed because we know that in real life objects don't appear or vanish into thin air. We know that you can't turn something into nothing or nothing into something. Without realizing it, we're using the Law of Conservation of Matter.

The Law of Conservation of Matter is usually stated like this: Matter can neither be created nor destroyed. Matter, of course, is stuff. Any kind of stuff—solid, liquid, or gas. The Law of Conservation of Matter says that whatever anyone does to an object, the matter it is made of will continue to exist, in some form or another. This law is also known as the Law of Conservation of Mass. Mass is the measurement of the *amount* of matter that any object contains.

A rock is a piece of matter. Let's use it as an example. Suppose we hit our rock with a sledge hammer and break it into pieces. Is the rock still there? Of course. It has just changed form.

Let's grind our pieces of rock into a fine powder and toss it up into the wind. The powder blows away. Have we destroyed anything? No. The same amount of rock still exists, but now it has become tiny particles that are scattered far and wide.

Perhaps some of our rock powder falls into a farmer's field. A corn plant absorbs some of the minerals with its roots. The rock now becomes part of the corn plant, but it still exists. If we eat the corn, the minerals may become a part of our body. Still nothing has been destroyed.

Suppose we wanted to try these experiments, but we didn't have a rock. No matter where we looked, we just couldn't find a rock! Could we create one? Could we say some sort of magic spell that would make a rock appear from nowhere? Of course not. It seems very clear that matter cannot be created, either.

But grinding a rock into powder is just a physical change. No matter how fine we grind the rock, it's still rock. In chemical reactions, totally new substances are formed. For example, when

No matter how we change the form *of a rock, the material the rock is made of will never disappear.*

we mix vinegar and baking soda, carbon dioxide gas is formed. The gas wasn't there before the reaction took place. Has new matter been created? Has any of the vinegar or baking soda been destroyed?

Fire is one type of chemical reaction. Think about what happens when you burn a piece of paper. You start out with a full-sized sheet of paper, but after the flames die out, all that's left is a little pile of ash. If you weigh the paper before and after you burn it, you'll discover that the paper weighs much more than the ashes that are left behind. It certainly *looks* as though matter is destroyed by fire. If you had been a scientist in the early 1700s, this would have been one of your biggest puzzles.

There's another side to this same problem. Scientists in the 1700s also knew that if you heated certain chemicals, such as iron powder or mercury, they would change appearance and get heavier! It seemed that new matter was being created as they heated the metals.

It took one of the world's great scientists, Antoine Lavoisier, to figure out what was happening. And it is the Frenchman Lavoisier who is given credit for first stating the Law of Conservation of Matter.

Before Lavoisier, scientists explained that objects lost weight when they burned because they combined with a substance in the air called *phlogiston*. Phlogiston was supposed to have negative weight, and so a burning substance that combined with it would get lighter instead of heavier. Metals were supposed to give off phlogiston when heated, which explained why they got heavier. The trouble was, nobody had ever seen phlogiston or been able to collect it in a laboratory.

Lavoisier realized that the reason no one could find any phlogiston was because it wasn't there. He discovered that when things burn, they combine with oxygen, a gas in the air. Sometimes this burning creates other gases. The gases blow away, leaving only a little bit of ash. It might look as though matter has been destroyed, but actually it has simply changed form, become a gas, and entered the atmosphere. If you carefully trapped and weighed all the gases that were produced when a sheet of paper burned, you would find that all the matter from that paper still existed.

Lavoisier heated measured amounts of mercury and iron in closed containers and noted that they changed to rustlike substances as he did. These reddish substances (oxides) weighed more than the original metals. But there was also less air inside the closed containers. The amount of air that had been used up was equal to the amount of weight that the metals had gained. Lavoisier realized that no new matter had been created. Instead, the metals had combined with a portion of the air, which Lavoisier called *oxygen*. After many experiments, Lavoisier was sure that, while substances might change form or combine with other substances, matter could not be created or destroyed in ordinary chemical reactions.

Of course, when you mix vinegar and baking soda, nothing is created or destroyed, either. The two chemicals react with each other, forming other substances, including carbon dioxide

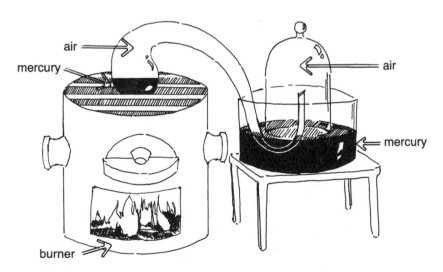

Lavoisier heated mercury in a sealed container to prove that matter is neither created nor destroyed.

gas. The same amount of material is still there. It has simply changed form.

Why was the Law of Conservation of Matter so important? If scientists knew that matter couldn't be created or destroyed, they could weigh their chemicals carefully, conduct their experiments, and figure out how elements combine to form various compounds. Only after Lavoisier and others realized that matter couldn't be created or destroyed could chemistry become an exact science. For this and other great contributions, Lavoisier is usually known as the founder of modern chemistry.

10.

PASCAL'S LAW—HOW LIQUIDS BEHAVE

If you are a good swimmer, you've probably tried swimming down to the bottom of a pool or lake. When you did, you certainly felt the water pushing harder on you as you swam deeper and deeper. If you were wearing goggles, you felt the water pressing them firmly against your face. Water can exert a tremendous amount of pressure. In the deepest parts of the ocean, the pressure of the water is more than 16,000 pounds per square inch!

Ever since the earliest civilizations, humans have needed dependable supplies of water. We need water to drink, to wash, to grow our crops, and to supply us with power. But to use water effectively, we have to learn how water behaves and how it can be controlled. We need to know the laws that explain how water flows and water pressure works.

The study of the behavior of liquids is known as *hydrodynamics*. The prefix *hydro-* means *water*, and *dynamics* is the study of motion. One of the earliest and most important laws of hydrodynamics is known as Pascal's Law.

Pascal's Law is named for its discoverer, Blaise Pascal, a French scientist and philosopher who lived and worked in the mid-1600s. Pascal's scientific studies focused on pressure, in both liquids and gases. He was the first to prove that air pressure decreased with altitude. Pascal was sickly throughout his short life, but his friends climbed high into the mountains for him and took barometer readings at different heights. The different measurements they recorded proved that air pressure is greatest at sea level and that it becomes less as the altitude increases.

Gravity pulls the air of our atmosphere down toward the center of the Earth. Air pressure is caused by the weight of the atmosphere pressing down from above. At higher altitudes the air is thinner. There is less air pressing down, and so the air pressure is less.

Pascal knew that something very similar happens with water pressure. In any container of water, the pressure is least at the top. As you go deeper and deeper in the water, the pressure increases. The deeper you go, the more water there is above, pressing down. This is true in a drinking glass, a swimming pool, or an ocean.

To demonstrate this for yourself, all you need is an empty plastic jug. Using a small nail, carefully punch a series of three or four holes down the side of the jug. The first hole should be near the top of the jug, and the last should be very near the bottom. Now fill the jug with water and watch it squirt out of the holes. You'll see that the water barely dribbles out of the top hole. But water coming out of the holes farther down the side spurts out more and more forcefully. The lower-most hole has the strongest stream of all. That is because the water at that point is the deepest and has the greatest pressure.

The additional pressure is caused by the weight of the water above pressing down. The amount of water above a point is known as the *water column*. The deeper a point is, the taller the column of water above it. The water in that column presses down with all its weight. And water is heavy! One gallon of water weighs more than 8 pounds. A cubic meter (a cube 1 meter long, 1 meter wide, and 1 meter high) of water has a mass of 1,000 kilograms, or about a ton.

Water pressure depends only on the *depth* of the water column. The total *amount* of water in a container and the shape of the container make no difference. At a depth of 10 meters, there is exactly as much water pressure in a narrow pipe and a 10-

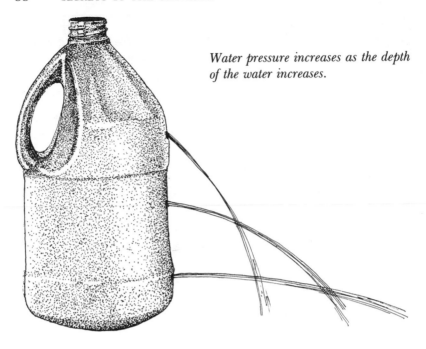

Water pressure increases as the depth of the water increases.

million-gallon lake. In the drawing below, the pressure at the bottom of each container would be exactly the same.

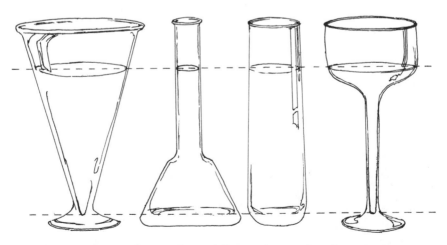

Although the containers have different shapes, the water pressure at the bottom of each one is exactly the same.

Pascal proved this by making a container that looked like this:

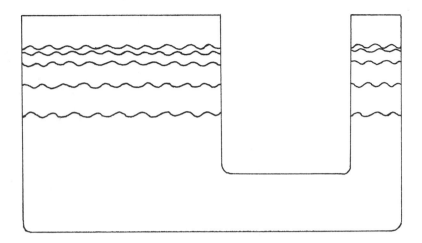

Pascal built this container to show that water pressure depends on the depth, not the size or shape of the container.

You might think that section *A* would have more pressure, because it contains more water. But if section *A* had more pressure, then we would expect that pressure to push the water up higher in section *B*. When Pascal filled his container with water, the smaller column of water reached exactly the same height as the larger one. That meant that the pressures had to be equal.

If you have a teakettle or pitcher with a spout in your kitchen at home, you can perform a similar experiment. Fill the pitcher with water. The water in the spout will always be at exactly the same level as the water in the larger portion of the pitcher.

Perhaps you have heard the expression "Water seeks its own level." Pascal's experiment shows the reason for that: Equal columns of a liquid exert equal pressures.

Water pressure at any point is directly proportional to the depth of the water at that point. The deeper the water, the greater the pressure. But Pascal found that water pressure doesn't just push downward. If that were true, then whenever we dived underwater, we would be pushed right to the bottom! That doesn't happen, of course. Water pressure pushes in all directions equally.

To demonstrate this fact, you will need a bucket and a couple of empty plastic drinking cups. Punch a hole in the bottom of one cup with a nail. Fill the bucket with water. Now push the cup partway down into the water. You should see water being pushed *up* through the hole in the bottom of the cup.

Try the same experiment with another cup. This time punch a hole in the side of the cup. Push this cup into the water. Notice the direction that the water takes as it gushes into the cup.

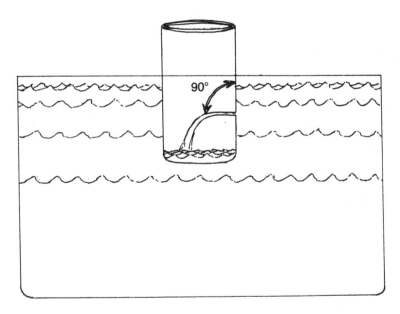

Water pressure pushes at right angles to the side of a container.

Pascal noticed that the pressure of a liquid always seems to push at 90 degrees to the object it is pushing against. With the hole in the bottom of the cup, the water pushed directly up. When the hole was in the side, the water pushed in sideways. Therefore, the pressure of a liquid pushes in *all* directions. And it always acts at right angles to the object it pushes against.

Pascal also considered what happens when you apply additional pressure to a liquid. When pressure is applied to a gas, the gas can be compressed into a smaller space. For example, scuba divers can squeeze an hour's worth of air into a small steel tank. But liquids can't be compressed. No matter how much pressure is applied to them, liquids will not squeeze into a smaller space.

Imagine you have a container like the one below.

Let's suppose the tube on the left has a piston that can be moved up or down. What will happen when you push down on that piston? The pressure you apply will be transmitted through the water, forcing the water level in the other tube to rise.

Pascal realized that when pressure is applied to a liquid in a container, that pressure doesn't remain just at the point where

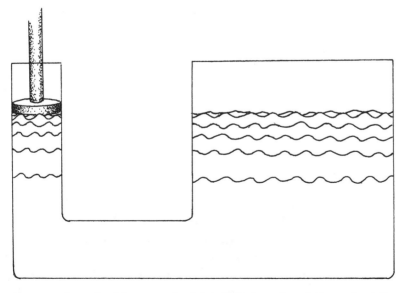

Pressure from the piston on the left will be transferred throughout the liquid.

it is applied. The pressure is distributed evenly throughout the liquid. That rule, combined with the idea that liquid pressure pushes evenly in all directions, is known as Pascal's Law. Pascal's Law can be stated like this: Pressure applied to a liquid at any point in a closed container is transmitted evenly throughout the container. The pressure always exerts a force at right angles to the walls of the container.

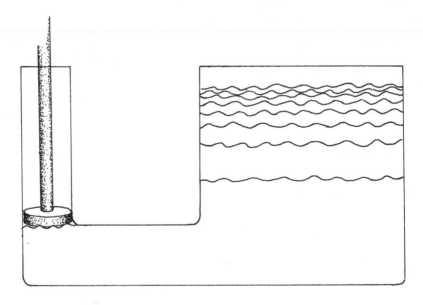

When you push down on the piston on the left, the water on the right rises.

Suppose we press down on the piston in the diagram with 1 kilogram of force per square centimeter. That pressure is distributed evenly throughout the container. Wherever we measure the pressure of the liquid, the reading will be the same: 1 kilogram per square centimeter.

Pascal's Law has some very important uses in our modern world. Imagine a container with one small piston and one large piston. Let's suppose that the small piston is 1 square centimeter

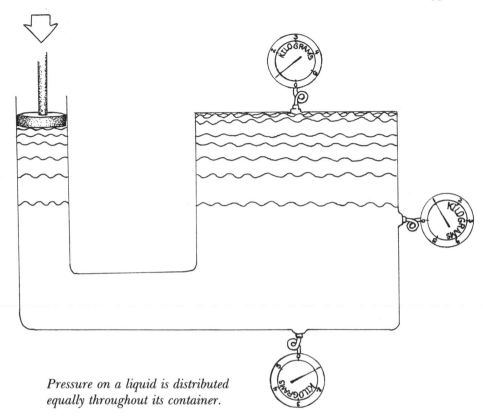

*Pressure on a liquid is distributed
equally throughout its container.*

in area, and the large piston has an area of 10 square centimeters. Then our container would look like this:

If you push down on the small piston with 1 kilogram of force, you are exerting a pressure of 1 kilogram per square centimeter. Pascal's Law tells us that the liquid in the container will transmit that amount of pressure everywhere in the container. Each square centimeter will have 1 kilogram of pressure on it.

Now look at the other piston. It has an area of 10 square centimeters. Pascal's Law says that pressure applied to a liquid is transmitted evenly throughout the container. So each square centimeter in our container must have 1 kilogram of pressure

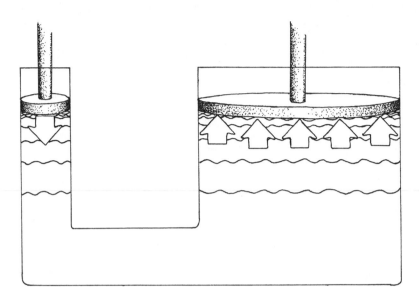

One kilogram of force on the smaller piston is multiplied to 10 kilograms of force on the larger one.

pushing on it. That means the large piston has a total of 10 kilograms of pressure pushing on it. We could move a 10-kilogram weight using 1 kilogram of force!

However, you should also notice that to move the large piston up 1 centimeter, you would have to push the small piston down 10 centimeters. No work gets done for free when you follow the laws of physics!

The device we have just looked at is a simplified version of a hydraulic jack. It is used to lift heavy weights. You are most likely to see one at a garage or service station, where it is used to lift cars and trucks. A hydraulic jack uses Pascal's Law to multiply a person's effort. It lets someone move a large amount of mass with only a small amount of force.

Pascal's Law is also used in the braking system of every car. A car's brake system is a hydraulic system similar to the hydraulic jack. The driver's brake pedal is connected to the brakes in the wheels by long tubes. The tubes are filled with a liquid.

When the driver presses down on the brake pedal, he pushes on a piston. That increases the pressure in the brake fluid. Pascal's Law tells us that a liquid transmits pressure throughout a closed container. The liquid in the brake system transmits the pressure of the driver's foot to the brakes themselves. The brakes clamp against the turning wheel, slowing the car.

Devices like hydraulic jacks and automobile brakes don't use water to transmit pressure. When water and steel are in contact

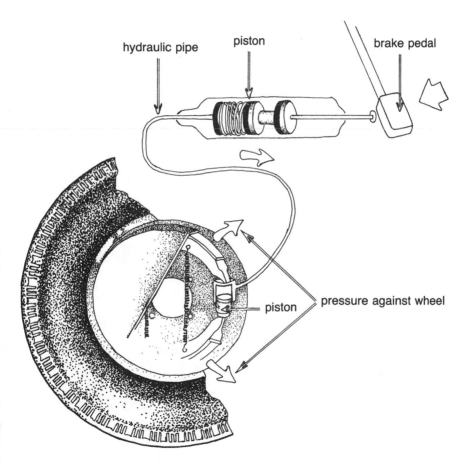

hydraulic pipe   piston   brake pedal

piston

pressure against wheel

A liquid in the automobile's brake system transmits force from the brake pedal to the wheels.

for long, the steel begins to rust. Instead, they use a kind of oil. Because the oil is a liquid, it also follows Pascal's Law.

Blaise Pascal was a genius who accomplished many things in his short life. He was a noted religious philosopher. He was the first scientist to create a vacuum in the laboratory. In addition to his pressure studies, Pascal is best known for his mathematical study of probability, or chance. He also built the first mechanical calculating machine. Pascal's machine is usually considered the first computer. In honor of that accomplishment, a modern-day computer language is named for him. And because of his achievements in the study of air and water pressure, the metric unit that is used to measure pressure is called the pascal.

11.

BOYLE'S AND CHARLES'S LAWS—HOW GASES BEHAVE

If you look at the directions on any aerosol spray can, you will see a warning: DO NOT INCINERATE. That means don't throw the can into a fire. If you do, the heat will turn that harmless spray can into a bomb.

What causes the heated can to explode so violently? Why does a rubber bicycle tire, when pumped up with enough soft, gentle air, become firm and hard? And why does the air released from the valve of that tire always feel cold, even on the hottest day? These events are explained by a set of rules called the *gas laws*.

Matter comes in three different forms, or states: solid, liquid, and gas. Most substances can exist in any of these three states, depending on its temperature. For example, water can exist as ice (solid), water (liquid), or water vapor (gas).

Each state of matter has different properties. A solid has a definite size and a definite shape. An ice cube, a brick, or a pencil holds its shape if we turn it or move it from one place to another. A liquid has a definite size but no particular shape. When we pour water or oil from one container to another, it changes shape to fit whatever container it is in. But it still takes up the same amount of space, even if we try to compress (squeeze) it.

A gas has the most interesting behavior of all. A gas has neither a definite shape nor a definite size. Air is a gas, of course. It can take the shape of a football, a basketball, or a bicycle tire. No matter what shape the container has, the gas will fit it.

A gas can expand to fill any size and shape of space. And a gas can be compressed (squeezed) into smaller volumes too. It will completely fill any container it is put in.

Picture a closed room with nothing in it, not even air. Such an empty space is called a vacuum. If we release a small amount of air into that room, it won't stay in just one place. It will quickly spread out and fill the whole room evenly.

We can fill a container with lots and lots of gas by putting it under pressure. You have certainly seen pressurized steel canisters of helium gas. We can then use the gas in one small container to fill hundreds of helium balloons. All together, the balloons take up much more space than the canister. But both were filled with the same amount of gas.

In the late 1600s the English scientist Robert Boyle invented an air pump. This pump could increase or decrease the amount of gas in a container. The pump could even remove almost the air from a container, creating a vacuum.

Boyle noticed that gas seemed to be "springy." The smaller the space he squeezed it into, the more pressure the gas had. He discovered that there was an exact relationship between the pressure of a gas and the volume of space it was squeezed into.

Picture a container of air. Imagine that we can compress the container of air to make it smaller, without any of the air inside escaping. If we compressed the container to half of its original size, the pressure of the air inside would be twice as great. If we squeezed the container to one-third of its original size, the pressure would be three times as great. Boyle also noticed that this rule is true only as long as the temperature of the gas is kept the same.

Boyle's Law is usually stated like this: At a constant temperature, the volume of a gas is inversely proportional to its pressure.

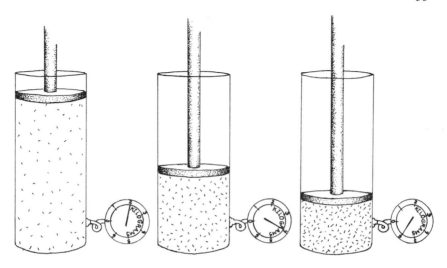

When a gas is squeezed into a smaller space, its pressure increases.

Remember that *inversely proportional* means that as the pressure on the gas increases, the volume decreases.

We often see Boyle's Law at work in our everyday world. Boyle's Law explains why a bicycle pump works. As you push down on the handle of a bicycle pump, the air inside is forced into a smaller and smaller space. As the air's volume decreases, its pressure increases. This increased pressure forces the air out of the pump's nozzle and into the tire you are inflating.

Boyle's Law also explains why basketballs and tennis balls are bouncy. The balls are filled with pressurized gas. When a basketball hits the floor, the bottom of the ball is pushed in slightly. That increases the pressure in the ball, because there is less space for the air inside. The pressure of the air pushes back against the flexible wall of the ball, making it spring back into the air.

Boyle's Law is even responsible for our breathing. When we breathe in, a muscle called the diaphragm moves. This increases the volume of our lungs. The extra volume means that our lungs have less air pressure than the outside air. The outside

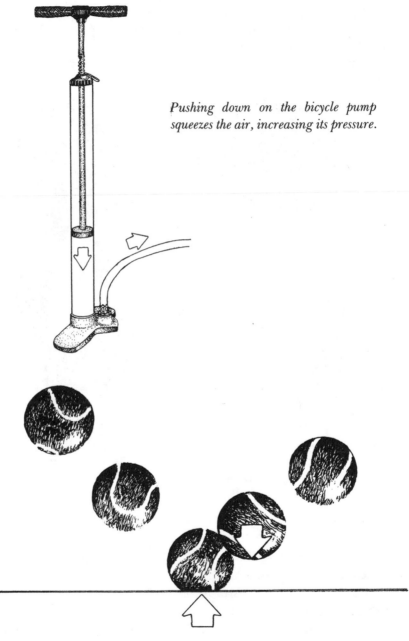

Pushing down on the bicycle pump squeezes the air, increasing its pressure.

A tennis ball gets most of its bounce from the compression of the gas inside it.

air, which has more pressure, rushes in to fill the extra space.
When we breath out, the diaphragm decreases the volume of
our lungs. That raises the pressure, forcing the air to rush
out again.

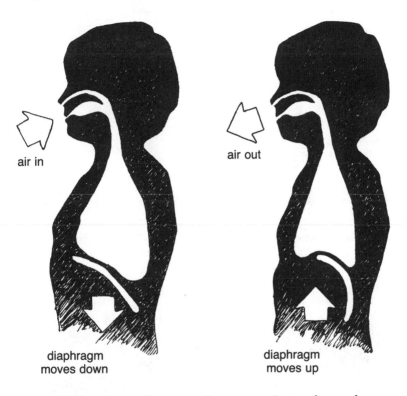

air in

air out

diaphragm
moves down

diaphragm
moves up

*As our diaphragm muscle moves, the pressure in our lungs changes,
and air moves in and out.*

Here's how to make a scientific toy called a Cartesian diver.
The Cartesian diver is named after the great French philosopher
and mathematician René Descartes. It works because of Boyle's
Law, along with Pascal's Law and Archimedes' Principle.

To make a Cartesian diver, you'll need a drinking glass, a
tall, narrow-mouthed, clear bottle, like a 2-liter soda bottle,
and a medicine dropper. If you don't have a medicine dropper
at home, you should be able to buy one at any drugstore.

Fill both the drinking glass and the bottle almost to the top with water. Carefully fill the medicine dropper with just enough water so that it *barely* floats at the surface of the water in the drinking glass. If you use too much water, the dropper will sink. (That's why you should try it out in the drinking glass first, before you put it into the bottle.) If you use too little water, you won't be able to make it dive. Add or remove a few drops of water at a time until the diver floats, as shown in the diagram below.

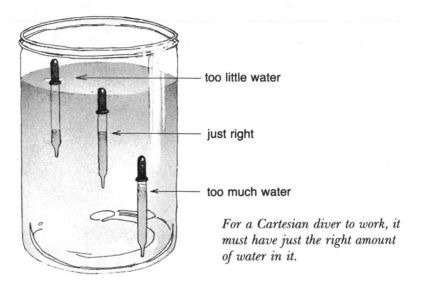

For a Cartesian diver to work, it must have just the right amount of water in it.

Once you have the right amount of water in the dropper, transfer it to the tall bottle. Be careful not to lose any water by squeezing the rubber bulb as you do this. Place the palm of your hand over the mouth of the bottle, making a tight seal. Hold the bottle steady with your other hand.

Now press down on the mouth of the bottle with the palm of your hand. The medicine dropper should dive to the bottom of the bottle. It will stay there as long as you keep the pressure on the top of the bottle. When you release the pressure, the diver should rise back to the surface.

It may take a little practice before you can make your diver

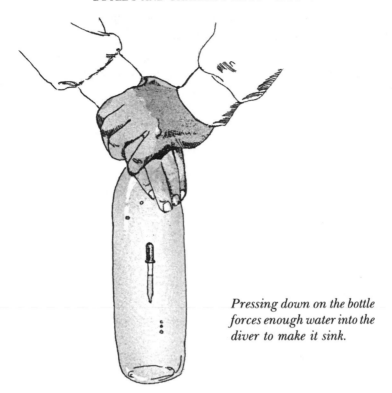

*Pressing down on the bottle
forces enough water into the
diver to make it sink.*

move up and down, but once you get the hang of it, it's easy!
You can even make the diver float in the middle of the bottle,
if you adjust the pressure of your hand correctly.

The Cartesian diver works because of three laws: The first
is Pascal's Law (Chapter 10). Remember that liquids cannot
be compressed into smaller spaces the way gases can. Pascal's
Law says that when pressure is applied to a liquid, the pressure
is transmitted evenly in all directions throughout the liquid.
That means that when your hand presses on the top of the
bottle, pressure increases *everywhere* inside the bottle.

Watch the diver very closely as you make it dive and sink
several times. You should notice something interesting happening to the water level inside the dropper. When you apply
pressure, a little more water goes up into the dropper. When
you release the pressure, the water level in the dropper goes

back down again. The pressure from your hand is transmitted through the water and pushes on the air in the dropper.

Boyle's Law tells us that when the pressure on a gas increases, its volume decreases. The water, pressing on the air in the dropper, squeezes it into a smaller space. That allows a little more water to enter the dropper.

When water enters the dropper, the dropper becomes slightly heavier. It becomes denser than the water around it, and so it sinks (Archimedes' Principle). When we release the pressure, the "springiness" of the air pushes the water back out again. Then the dropper is slightly lighter, just light enough to float back up.

A second rule about the behavior of gases was discovered about one hundred years after Boyle's Law. It is known as Charles's Law, after its first discoverer, the French scientist Jacques Charles. Charles was interested in scientific explorations through ballooning. He realized that gases expand when heated. In fact, that is what allows a hot-air balloon to rise.

Although it was Charles who first noticed that gases expand with heat, it was actually two other scientists who first stated the law that is now named after him. Those scientists were the Englishman John Dalton and the Frenchman Joseph Louis Gay-Lussac. Charles's Law is usually stated: If the volume of a gas remains constant, the pressure of the gas is directly proportional to its temperature.

As the temperature of a gas increases, its pressure increases. Charles's Law also tells us that if the *pressure* of a gas stays the same, then the *volume* will increase when the gas is heated.

It's easy to see Charles's Law in action. You will need a rubber balloon and a tall glass bottle. Slip the mouth of the balloon over the mouth of the bottle, making a tight seal. Now warm the bottle by holding it in a pan of hot water. Watch what happens to the balloon.

It begins to inflate! As the temperature of the air in the

As the air in the bottle is warmed, it expands.

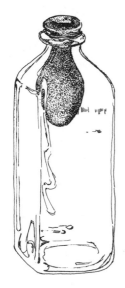

Cooling the air in the bottle causes it to contract.

bottle increases, its pressure increases. The extra pressure pushes some of the air out into the balloon, inflating it.

Take the bottle out of the hot water and allow it to cool. As the air in the bottle cools, the pressure drops and the balloon deflates. Try putting the bottle in the freezer. What do you think should happen? As the air in the bottle gets colder and colder, the pressure continues to decrease. The outside air pressure, which is greater, pushes the balloon into the bottle.

Charles's Law explains why an aerosol container in a fire is so dangerous. The pressure of the gases inside the can increases as the can gets hotter and hotter. Finally the can isn't strong enough to hold the pressure anymore, and it explodes.

Something very similar happens inside a gasoline engine. In each cylinder gasoline is mixed with air and then ignited with a spark. The gasoline explodes, creating a very rapid rise in temperature. The gases in the cylinder also expand rapidly because of the heat. This expansion provides the force that pushes the piston in the cylinder, providing the engine's power.

Automobile manuals always instruct drivers to check the air pressure in their tires when they are cold. As a car rolls along the highway, the friction of the tires against the road creates heat. Charles's Law tells us that as the tires get hotter, the pressure of the air inside them increases. When the car stops and the tires cool off, the pressure goes back down again.

A "blowout" is caused when a weakened tire can't hold the pressure of the air inside it. Blowouts almost always happen while a car is moving rapidly. The friction of rapid motion heats up the tires. That's when the pressure inside the tire is the greatest, according to Charles's Law.

In 1824 Gay-Lussac and another French scientist, Sadi Carnot, realized that Boyle's Law and Charles's Law could be combined. They put the two laws together into what is known as the Ideal Gas Law. The Ideal Gas Law says: The volume of a gas is directly proportional to its temperature and inversely proportional to its pressure. To figure out the volume of a gas, you need to know *both* its temperature and its pressure. The Ideal Gas Law is simply Boyle's and Charles's laws put together in a single statement. In mathematical form, it looks like this:

$$\text{Volume} = R \times \frac{\text{Temperature}}{\text{Pressure}} \qquad or \qquad V = R \times \frac{T}{P}$$

R stands for a special small number called the gas constant, which must be used to get exact measurements from the formula. The Ideal Gas Law simply says that the volume of a gas increases as the temperature increases, and decreases as the pressure increases.

This law has a very familiar and important use in our everyday lives. It is the reason our refrigerators, freezers, and air conditioners all work.

Have you ever touched the base of a bicycle pump after you have pumped up a tire? It is very hot. You may also have noticed that when you let air out of a bicycle or car tire, it always feels cold, even on the hottest day. If you have not felt cool air coming out of a tire valve, try it the next time you check the tires of your bike or family car at a service station.

The Ideal Gas Law tells us that when we force a gas into a smaller space, its temperature increases. It's the hot, compressed air that makes the bottom of the bicycle pump so hot. The Ideal Gas Law also tells us that when the pressure on a gas is decreased, the gas's temperature decreases. That's why the air released from a tire always feels cool.

Now picture a gas-pumping machine with two parts. One part compresses the gas, making it hotter. The other part releases the pressure, allowing it to cool. That is a refrigerator.

Every refrigerator has tubes, called coils. In some refrigerators and freezers you can see the coils. They are the winding metal tubes often covered with frost. In these coils a pressurized gas is allowed to release its pressure. When that happens, the gas becomes cooler. This takes place inside an insulated box that we call the refrigerator. As the gas gets cooler, it absorbs heat and cools whatever is in the box too.

After the gas has cooled the inside of the refrigerator, it is pumped outside the insulated box. There a machine called a compressor, driven by an electric motor, repressurizes the gas. As the gas is pressurized, it gets hotter. But since the compressor is *outside* the insulated box, the heat doesn't warm the food back up. Instead, the excess heat (which the gas absorbed inside the refrigerator) is picked up by the surrounding air. Usually a small fan keeps air circulating around the compressor to take away the heat. The repressurized gas is then circulated back inside the refrigerator for more cooling.

If you get close enough to your refrigerator, you should be able to hear the compressor motor running and feel the heat that has been removed from the pressurized gas. Freezers and air conditioners work in exactly the same way. They are all

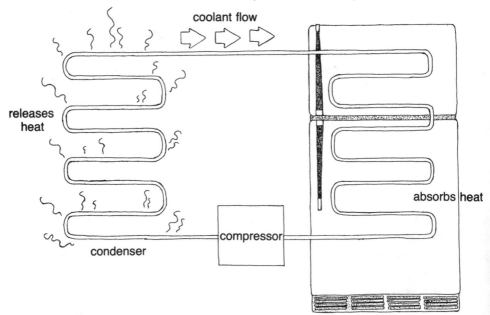

Compressed gas in the coils removes heat from the insulated refrigerator, and releases it to the surrounding air.

"heat pumps." Thanks to the Ideal Gas Law, they pump heat out of an area to be cooled and into the surrounding air.

Boyle's and Charles's laws were important in the history of science because they provided strong evidence for the existence of atoms. Here's why.

Scientists picture a gas as made up of many tiny moving particles, or molecules. As gas molecules are packed closer together in a smaller space, it makes sense that more of them collide with the walls of their container. More tiny collisions result in more pressure. Boyle's Law tells us that this is exactly what happens. A gas increases in pressure when its volume is decreased.

In the 1800s scientists also realized that heat energy is actually the motion of atoms and molecules. The hotter a substance is, the faster its particles move. Charles' Law supports this idea. The faster the gas molecules are moving, the harder their collisions with the walls of their container should be. Harder collisions mean more pressure. And that is exactly what happens. As a gas gets hotter, it does have more pressure.

In 1860 the British scientist James Clerk Maxwell showed that Boyle's and Charles's laws resulted from the motion of gas molecules. This proved that heat is the energy of molecular motion. The hotter something is, the faster its molecules move.

One other result of the gas laws is also very important and interesting. Starting at 0 degrees Celsius, any gas loses $\frac{1}{273}$ of its volume for each degree it is cooled. Since heat is actually the motion of molecules, that means that when a gas is cooled 1 degree, it loses $\frac{1}{273}$ of its molecular motion.

In 1848 William Thomson, Lord Kelvin, realized that if a gas were cooled to -273 degrees C, its molecules would stop moving completely! That temperature, when all motion stops, is called absolute zero. As far as we know, there is no upper limit to how hot matter can get. But Lord Kelvin proved that there is a limit to coldness. At -273 degrees C all molecules stop moving. Matter just can't get any colder than that.

12.

BERNOULLI'S PRINCIPLE

Did you ever wonder how an airplane gets off the ground? A big jetliner weighs hundreds of thousands of pounds. How can something that heavy manage to fly? The answer is Bernoulli's Principle, a law discovered by the Swiss mathematician Daniel Bernoulli in 1738.

To see Bernoulli's Principle in action, cut a strip from a page of a newspaper. The strip should be about 5 centimeters (about 2 inches) wide and at least 30 centimeters (about 1 foot) long. Hold one end of the paper strip just below your lips and blow lightly over the paper.

hold
paper here

To see Bernoulli's principle at work,
blow gently across a strip of paper.

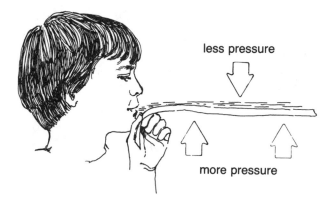

less pressure

more pressure

The faster-moving air above the paper has less pressure, and so the paper rises.

You probably expected the paper to be forced down by your breath, but instead, the paper rose! That's Bernoulli's Principle at work. Bernoulli's Principle says that the pressure of a gas or liquid decreases as its velocity increases.

In the experiment you just tried, the air above the paper was moving fast because you were blowing. The air below the strip of paper was still. That means the moving air above the paper had less pressure than the air below it. Since there was more pressure below the paper than above it, the paper was pushed upward.

The same principle that caused the paper to rise also gives airplanes their "lift." If you look at a cross-section of an airplane wing, it looks like this:

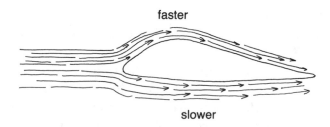

faster

slower

The special shape of an airfoil gives airplane wings their lift.

This special shape is called an *airfoil*. As the wing moves through the air, some air passes over the wing and some passes under it. Because the airfoil is curved on top, the air passing over the wing has a longer distance to travel in the same amount of time. That means it has to move slightly faster than the air passing underneath the wing.

Bernoulli's Principle tells us that when a gas moves faster, it has less pressure. Since air is moving faster over the wing than under it, there is less pressure above and more pressure below. That gives the wing lift. If the airplane has been designed correctly, it gives enough lift to get the plane off the ground and keep it airborne.

Moving the plane forward forces air to blow over the wings and creates that lift. The force that moves a jet airplane forward comes as a result of Newton's Third Law of Motion (Chapter 5). The *action* of the engine pushes huge quantities of exhaust gases backward. As a *reaction*, the plane goes forward. As it moves faster and faster, the wind blowing over the wings finally creates enough lift to get the plane off the ground.

Bernoulli's Principle works just as well with liquids. Most chemistry labs have a piece of equipment called an aspirator. Chemists use an aspirator when they need small amounts of suction. An aspirator attaches to a water faucet and looks like this:

When the water is turned on, it rushes past the side tube at a high speed. According to Bernoulli's Principle, high velocity creates low pressure. So the side tube generates suction as air or liquid flows in the direction of the arrows toward the low pressure area. If you put your finger at the end of the side tube, you would be able to feel the suction created by this pressure difference.

The type of garden bug sprayer that attaches to the end of a garden hose works the same way. The rapidly moving water creates an area of low pressure. This lower pressure gradually draws the chemicals up from the reservoir and into the spray directed toward the plants.

suction

The lower pressure of the flowing water creates suction in the tube at the side.

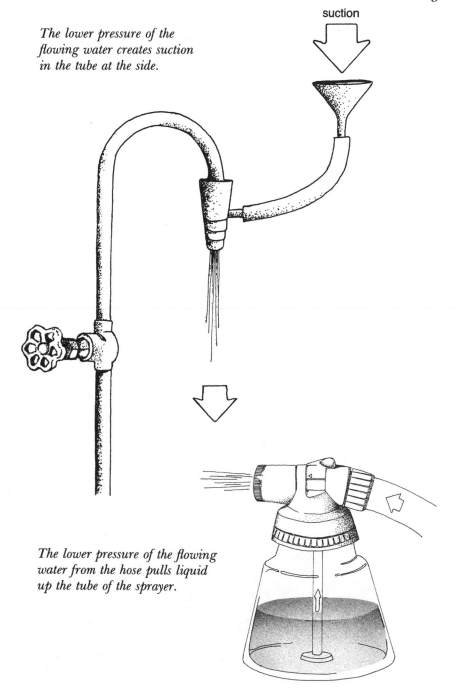

The lower pressure of the flowing water from the hose pulls liquid up the tube of the sprayer.

For one more amazing demonstration of Bernoulli's Principle, you'll need a strong blow dryer and a Ping-Pong ball. Plug in the dryer, turn it on high, and gently place the Ping-Pong ball in the stream of air.

The moving air should hold the Ping-Pong ball securely in place. You should be able to tilt the stream of air over to one side and still support the ball in the airstream. It looks as if gravity should make the ball fall, but instead the ball hangs mysteriously in midair.

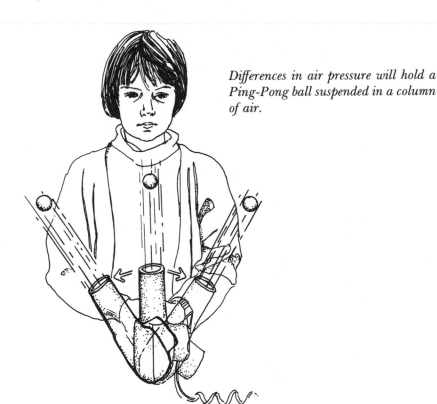

Differences in air pressure will hold a Ping-Pong ball suspended in a column of air.

Try it. Can you figure out just what is holding the ball in place?

The Ping-Pong ball is surrounded by a column of rapidly moving air. That air has low pressure, according to Bernoulli's

Principle. Surrounding the moving air is still air, with higher pressure. Whenever the ball starts to move out of the moving air column, the higher pressure in the surrounding air pushes it back. The ball is light enough and the pressure difference is strong enough to overcome the force of gravity for a time. Gravity is still working, of course. It's just that in this case, the force of Bernoulli's Principle is stronger. The same thing is true every time a huge jetliner lifts off a runway.

13.

HOW THE ELEMENTS COMBINE—THE LAW OF DEFINITE PROPORTIONS AND GAY-LUSSAC'S LAW

Suppose you broke a stone into smaller and smaller pieces. How far could you go before you reached the smallest possible piece of material? And when the rock was finally broken into its smallest parts, what would be left?

Just what *is* matter made of? In ancient times, philosophers thought that everything on Earth was composed of just four elements: earth, air, fire, and water. They believed that everything we see around us was made of those four substances, combined in different proportions.

In the 1700s chemists realized that our planet was made of more than earth, air, fire, and water after all. But the idea of elements remained. After experimenting with many different materials, chemists found that most things they tested could be broken down into other substances. But they also found a small number of special substances that could never be broken down into anything else. These substances became known as *elements*. By the late 1700s chemists had identified about twenty-five elements, including gold, silver, copper, iron, lead, sulfur, hydrogen, oxygen, and nitrogen.

The elements are the "building blocks" of all the other substances on Earth, called *compounds*. For example, iron and oxygen combine to form a reddish powder, iron oxide, or rust. Hydrogen and oxygen combine to form the compound water.

Calcium, carbon, and oxygen combine to form calcium carbonate, or chalk. Chemists can make iron oxide or water or calcium carbonate in their laboratories by mixing the correct elements together and then heating them or by following some other procedure.

Chemists can also reverse the process, separating compounds into their elements. For example, iron oxide can be heated in a furnace until the two elements that compose it are separated. Oxygen is released as a gas, leaving pure metallic iron in the container that held the rust.

But there is something special about the way the elements combine with one another to form compounds. You can't just mix elements together in any amount to form compounds. The elements combine only in certain, regular proportions by weight.

For example, 1 gram of hydrogen gas will always combine with exactly 8 grams of oxygen gas to form 9 grams of water. Hydrogen and oxygen gases *always* combine in the proportion of 1 to 8 by weight. If there is extra oxygen or extra hydrogen in the reaction, it will be left over. If you try combining 1 gram of hydrogen with 12 grams of oxygen, the result will still be 9 grams of water, with 4 grams of oxygen left over.

All other chemical reactions work the same way. Chemical elements always combine with one another in certain definite proportions. Copper and oxygen combine to form a compound called cuprous oxide. Cuprous oxide always has 4 grams of copper to every 1 gram of oxygen. Copper combines with carbon and oxygen to form a compound called copper carbonate. Copper carbonate always has 5 grams of copper to every 4 grams of oxygen and 1 gram of carbon.

The French chemist Joseph Proust was the first to notice that chemicals always combine in this very regular way. He experimented with many different compounds. In every reaction the elements always combined with each other in regular amounts. If he used too much of one element, the extra would be left over. In 1797, as a result of his experiments, Proust

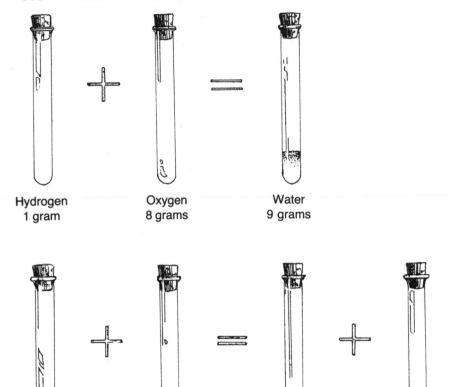

Hydrogen	Oxygen	Water	
1 gram	8 grams	9 grams	

Hydrogen	Oxygen	Water	Oxygen
1 gram	12 grams	9 grams	4 grams

One gram of hydrogen combines with exactly 8 grams of oxygen to form 9 grams of water.

stated his Law of Definite Proportions: Elements always combine in definite proportions by weight.

Although it was Proust who first stated the Law of Definite Proportions, it was the English chemist John Dalton who discovered what the law meant. Elements always combine in definite proportions because each element is made up of many tiny, indivisible particles, each with a definite size and weight. Dalton

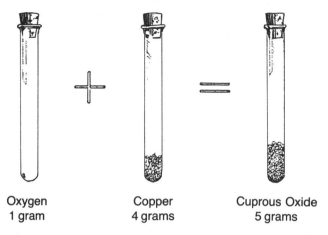

Oxygen   Copper   Cuprous Oxide
1 gram   4 grams   5 grams

To form cuprous oxide, copper and oxygen always combine in the ratio of 4 to 1.

called these smallest particles *atoms.* Four grams of copper always combine with 1 gram of oxygen. So, Dalton reasoned, the smallest particles of copper must be 4 times heavier than the smallest particles of oxygen. If you try to use more than 1 gram of oxygen to combine with 4 grams of copper in the reaction, there won't be enough copper atoms to combine with the extra oxygen. Some oxygen will be left over.

In 1808 Dalton declared that every element is made up of atoms. Atoms are the smallest possible particles of each element. They are much too small to be seen, even with a microscope. Dalton believed that all the atoms of a certain element must be exactly alike. The reason that each element is different, he said, is because its atoms are different from those of other elements. The atoms of one element all have the same weight. And the atoms of different elements have different weights.

Dalton and his fellow chemists pictured atoms as tiny balls with some sort of glue or hooks that allow them to combine with other atoms to form compounds.

Hydrogen is the lightest element. Dalton compared the weights of all the other known elements to the weight of hydrogen. He calculated an atomic weight for each known element. Dalton's calculations of atomic weights were not perfect, but they were useful in explaining why the elements always combine in definite proportions.

Dalton knew that under different conditions, some elements combine with others in more than one way. For example, carbon and oxygen can combine to form two different gases. In one gas the proportion of carbon to oxygen is 8 to 3. In the other gas the proportion is 8 to 6.

Copper can also combine with oxygen in two different ways. When these two elements combine in the proportion 4 to 1, the result is one compound. When they combine in the proportion of 8 to 1, a very different chemical compound is formed. How can that be?

Dalton realized that when elements combine with each other in several different ways, the Law of Definite Proportions still holds true. Elements still combine in certain proportions. It is just that several different proportions are sometimes possible. Dalton called this the Law of Multiple Proportions.

Dalton showed that his idea of atoms explained the Law of Multiple Proportions very well. If one atom of oxygen combines with one atom of carbon, the proportion of their weights will be 8 to 3. The gas produced is carbon monoxide (the prefix *mono-* means *one*).

If the number of atoms of oxygen is doubled, the proportion of carbon to oxygen will be 8 to 6. Then there will be two atoms of oxygen for each carbon atom. The gas produced in this reaction is carbon dioxide (the prefix *di-* means *two*). The Law of Multiple Proportions simply says that atoms can combine with one another in different ways, but they still always combine in definite proportions.

About the same time, the French chemist Joseph Gay-Lussac made a discovery that strongly supported Dalton's atomic ideas. Gay-Lussac was interested in the chemical reactions between different gases. For example, hydrogen gas and oxygen gas

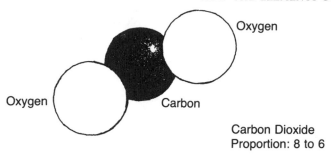

Carbon Dioxide
Proportion: 8 to 6

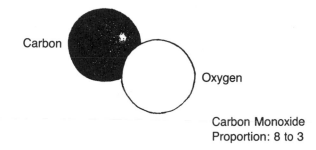

Carbon Monoxide
Proportion: 8 to 3

Carbon atoms can combine with either 1 or 2 oxygen atoms, forming either carbon monoxide or carbon dioxide.

combine to form water. And water can be separated into the two gases, hydrogen and oxygen.

Water is separated by passing an electric current through it. This process is called *electrolysis*. Gay-Lussac noticed that when water is separated into the two gases that compose it, the volume (*not weight*) of hydrogen is exactly twice as much as the volume of oxygen. For every liter of oxygen that is produced, there will be 2 liters of hydrogen.

The hydrogen gas from the electrolysis of water takes up exactly twice as much space as the oxygen. So Gay-Lussac reasoned that there had to be twice as many atoms of hydrogen as there were atoms of oxygen in the other container. Each water molecule was broken apart into two atoms of hydrogen and one atom of oxygen.

When you break water apart, you get twice as much hydrogen

as oxygen. But there are twice as many hydrogen atoms too. So in equal volumes of the gases, there have to be equal numbers of particles. That discovery became known as Gay-Lussac's Law. It is also known as Avogadro's Law, after the Italian chemist Amedeo Avogadro, who also studied how gases combine to form compounds.

Gay-Lussac found that other chemical reactions between gases follow the same rule: In chemical reactions gases always combine in simple proportions by volume. Hydrogen and oxygen combine in the proportion 2 to 1 to form water. Ammonia is made up of one atom of nitrogen and three atoms of hydrogen. If ammonia is broken up into its component elements, there will be 3 volumes of hydrogen for every 1 volume of nitrogen.

Remember that Boyle's and Charles' laws tell us that temperature and pressure affect the volume of gas in a container. So temperature and pressure must remain constant for Gay-Lussac's Law to be true. With that idea included, Gay-Lussac's Law is stated like this: If pressure and temperature remain constant, equal volumes of gas contain equal numbers of gas particles.

Knowing Gay-Lussac's Law helped chemists determine the exact composition of many compounds that are made with gaseous elements like oxygen, hydrogen, or nitrogen. But more importantly, Gay-Lussac's Law was evidence that Dalton was right when he said that all elements are composed of atoms.

You can see Gay-Lussac's Law in action by doing a fairly simple experiment. In this experiment you will use electrolysis to separate water into the two elements that it is composed of, hydrogen and oxygen. Because this experiment involves a tiny explosion, you should try it only when an adult is available to help.

You will need a lantern battery and some insulated wire, a deep baking pan, two test tubes or very small glasses (both the same size), table salt, and two small *aluminum* nails. You should be able to find aluminum nails at any hardware store.

Fill the baking pan about two-thirds full with water. Pour ¼ teaspoon of table salt (sodium chloride) into the water and stir until the salt dissolves. Adding salt improves the water's ability to conduct electricity.

Strip the insulation off both ends of two pieces of wire. Wrap one end of each piece of wire around an aluminum nail. Place the nails in the water at opposite ends of the baking pan. These two metal pieces are called *electrodes.*

Now put one test tube in the pan and fill it completely with water. Turn it upside down underwater so that none of the water in the tube escapes. Carefully put the glass tube over one of the electrodes. Repeat the same process with the other glass, placing it over the other electrode. Now connect the other ends of the wires to the battery terminals. Soon you should start to see bubbles of gas forming on the electrodes.

The gas bubbling from the positive electrode is oxygen, and the gas on the negative electrode is hydrogen. The bubbles of gas will gradually fill up the test tubes, forcing the water out. When the tube of hydrogen is completely full, look at the tube that is collecting the oxygen. It should be exactly half full.

Remember that Gay-Lussac's Law says that equal numbers of gas molecules will occupy equal volumes, if pressure and

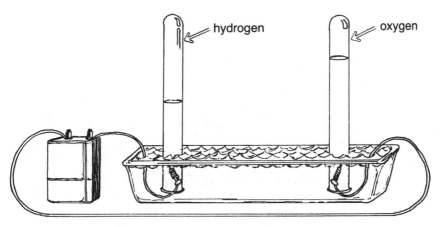

Water can be separated into hydrogen and oxygen gases using this simple equipment.

temperature remain constant. In your experiment the pressures and temperatures of the two test tubes are equal. There is twice as much hydrogen as there is oxygen. That tells us that water is composed of two hydrogen atoms for every oxygen atom.

How can we be certain which gases we have collected? We can test them. Hydrogen and oxygen are both odorless, colorless gases. Both gases you have produced meet that test.

Oxygen sustains burning. Tightly cover or cork the mouth of the test tube over the positive electrode while it is still underwater. Take the tube out of the water. Light a toothpick with a match. When it is burning well, blow it out. Quickly uncover the tube of gas and poke the glowing toothpick in. Be careful not to get it wet as you do. If you have collected oxygen, the toothpick will glow brightly and may even burst back into flame!

Hydrogen has a different property. It burns rapidly in air. Tightly seal the other tube underwater and remove it from the pan. Light another toothpick. Hydrogen is very light, and so this time hold the tube of gas upside down. That will prevent it from escaping when you open the tube. Uncover the tube and quickly put the burning toothpick to its mouth. You should hear a popping sound as the hydrogen you have collected explodes.

Dalton's ideas, supported by the findings of Gay-Lussac, Avogadro, and others, formed the basis of modern chemistry: Each element is made of vast numbers of tiny atoms, far too small for us to see. The atoms of each element combine with atoms of other elements to form the millions of compounds that our world is made of.

More recently scientists studying the light from distant stars have found that the very same elements that make up the Earth make up the rest of the universe as well. Throughout the universe, atoms of the different elements combine with one another in definite proportions, just as Proust, Dalton, Gay-Lussac, and others showed us almost two hundred years ago.

14.

MENDELEEV'S PERIODIC LAW

Elements are the building blocks of the universe. Each element is different from every other element. All the substances found on Earth, and everywhere else in the universe, are composed of individual elements or combinations of elements.

Each element is made up of atoms. The atoms of each element are all alike and are different from the atoms of every other element. John Dalton showed that the atoms of each element have their own particular atomic weight. And, of course, each element has its own unique set of properties.

By 1860 chemists had identified and studied over sixty different elements. But as chemists studied the elements, they noticed that each element also has similarities to some of the other elements.

There are many different ways that elements can be similar. For example, some elements are gases. Others are metallic. Some, like hydrogen, oxygen, sodium, and chlorine, are very reactive. They combine rapidly and easily in many chemical reactions. Some of these are so reactive that they are never found in their uncombined pure form on Earth. Other elements, like gold, platinum, and nitrogen, are more *inert*. They don't combine so easily with other elements. Those elements are found here on Earth in their elemental form (like gold nuggets or nitrogen gas).

Scientists always look for patterns in nature. As more and

more elements were discovered, it began to look as if there must be some sort of pattern among the elements. But what was that pattern?

The first thing that chemists looked at was atomic weight. Dalton had shown that the atoms of each element are different in weight. Chemists carefully calculated the atomic weight of each element. Since oxygen is a very common element that combines with most other elements, it was used as the standard measure of weight. All other elements were weighed by comparing them to the weight of oxygen.

All the known chemical elements could then be arranged in order by weight. Once that was done, chemists began examining the physical and chemical properties of the elements, looking for a pattern.

The chemical properties of the elements were most important in this search. All the elements known at that time reacted with other elements to form compounds. But each element only combines with others in certain ways. Chemists gave each element a particular combining number, or *valence,* based on the way it joins with other elements.

Here are just a few examples: One oxygen atom combines with two hydrogen atoms to form water. So each hydrogen atom is said to have a valence of 1, and the oxygen atom has a valence of 2. That is because the one oxygen atom can combine with *two* hydrogens. One atom of oxygen will combine with one atom of calcium to form calcium oxide. So the calcium atom, like the oxygen, must have a valence of 2. One nitrogen atom combines with three hydrogen atoms to form ammonia. Since each hydrogen atom has a combining power of 1, then nitrogen's valence must be 3.

But valence is only one of many properties that each element has. How did all those properties fit into one simple pattern? One chemist thought that all the elements with similar properties could be placed in groups of three. Another scientist thought every sixteenth element might be similar. Many different nu-

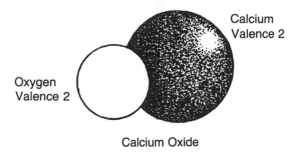

Calcium
Valence 2

Oxygen
Valence 2

Calcium Oxide

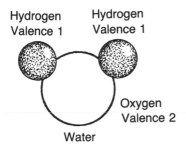

Hydrogen
Valence 1

Hydrogen
Valence 1

Oxygen
Valence 2

Water

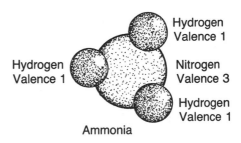

Hydrogen
Valence 1

Hydrogen
Valence 1

Nitrogen
Valence 3

Hydrogen
Valence 1

Ammonia

Valence numbers are based on the proportions in which different elements combine with one another.

merical arrangements were tried. But in every scheme, some elements just didn't fit properly.

Here is a list, by weight, of the first twenty elements known in the 1860s, along with their valences.

ELEMENT	VALENCE
Hydrogen	1
Lithium	1
Beryllium	2
Boron	3
Carbon	4
Nitrogen	3
Oxygen	2
Fluorine	1
Sodium	1
Magnesium	2
Aluminum	3
Silicon	4
Phosphorus	3
Sulfur	2
Chlorine	1
Potassium	1
Calcium	2
Titanium	3

In 1866 John Newlands suggested that the elements followed a pattern like a musical scale. The combining numbers or valences seemed to repeat themselves in groups of seven. Newlands published a chart of elements arranged in this pattern. The chart worked beautifully for the lighter elements listed above. But the pattern fell apart with the heavier elements. Newlands was on the right track, but he hadn't solved the puzzle.

In 1869 Dmitri Mendeleev, a Russian chemist, finally won the honor of discovering the pattern of the elements. Mendeleev realized that the valences of the elements are their most important chemical property. They show exactly how each element reacts with all other elements. Mendeleev arranged the elements according to their atomic weight. He then grouped them according to their valences. When he arranged the elements this way, he discovered that their chemical and physical properties showed a *periodic*, or repeating, pattern.

Newlands and the other chemists had tried to find a "magic

number" of elements that repeated again and again through the list of known elements. But Mendeleev didn't try to force the elements into a regular numerical pattern.

When Mendeleev got to the fourth repetition of the periodic cycle, he found a large number of elements in the list that had a valence of 3. Mendeleev simply made the period longer. Those "extra" elements all had to be included before the cycle continued. The same thing was true for the fifth period and sixth period. Because he grouped the elements by their properties, rather than any particular number, Mendeleev simply widened his chart to make room for the additional elements that belonged in those groups.

Mendeleev's discovery can be stated as a law: When arranged in order of atomic weight, the elements periodically repeat similar physical and chemical properties. This is known as the Periodic Law. Mendeleev's chart of the elements, which shows this repetition of properties, is known as the periodic table. The chart itself is actually the most complete statement of Mendeleev's law.

On page 130 is Mendeleev's original table, which included all the elements known to chemists of his time.

The elements in Mendeleev's chart are arranged by weight. Moving from left to right and down the page, the elements are in order by atomic weight. Each row across the page is called a *period*. Each period represents one complete repetition of similar chemical and physical properties.

Elements with similar properties are arranged underneath one another in columns. Each column of elements in the periodic table represents a group of elements with similar properties. These groups of elements are sometimes called *families* of elements.

For example, the elements in the first column are known as the *alkali metals* family. This family includes hydrogen, lithium, sodium, potassium, rubidium, and cesium. These elements are all metallic. Even hydrogen acts like a metal at very low temperatures. They all have a valence of 1. These elements are all so

Mendeleev arranged all the elements known in his time into a chart called the periodic table.

1 Hydrogen																
3 Lithium	4 Beryllium											5 Boron	6 Carbon	7 Nitrogen	8 Oxygen	9 Fluorine
11 Sodium	12 Magnesium											13 Aluminum	14 Silicon	15 Phosphorus	16 Sulfur	17 Chlorine
19 Potassium	20 Calcium		22 Titanium	23 Vanadium	24 Chromium	25 Manganese	26 Iron	27 Cobalt	28 Nickel	29 Copper	30 Zinc			33 Arsenic	34 Selenium	35 Bromine
37 Rubidium	38 Strontium	39 Yttrium	40 Zirconium	41 Niobium	42 Molybdenum		44 Ruthenium	45 Rhodium	46 Palladium	47 Silver	48 Cadmium	49 Indium	50 Tin	51 Antimony	52 Tellurium	53 Iodine
55 Cesium	56 Barium	57 Lanthanum		73 Tantalum	74 Tungsten		76 Oxmium	77 Iridium	78 Platinum	79 Gold	80 Mercury	81 Thallium	82 Lead	83 Bismuth		
			90 Thorium		92 Uranium											

chemically active that, except for hydrogen gas, they are never found on Earth in their pure form. They are always combined with other elements in compounds.

The second column is another group of metals, known as the *alkaline earth metals.* They have a valence of 2. They are also very reactive, although not quite as reactive as the elements in the first column.

Across the chart in column 7 is a family of elements known as the *halogens.* The halogens are nonmetals that are also very chemically active. In fact, fluorine is the most reactive element of all. It is so active that it is almost impossible to produce and keep fluorine in its elemental form. It will even react with glass! The halogens also include the elements chlorine, bromine, and iodine. They all have a valence of 1 and react strongly with metals. They have strong, unpleasant odors and can be quite poisonous.

As Mendeleev arranged the elements by their properties, he found several places where an element seemed to be missing. Mendeleev was so convinced that his Periodic Law was correct that he left empty spaces in his chart for undiscovered elements that he thought should be there.

Mendeleev was familiar with the properties of the other elements in the family where he thought the missing elements belonged. He knew that the missing elements would have similar properties. So Mendeleev made a prediction. He predicted that four new elements would be found. He predicted what the properties of those elements would be. If those elements *were* found, they would prove that Mendeleev's Periodic Law was correct. If they were not, then Mendeleev was wrong, and some other arrangement was needed to describe the properties of the elements.

Five years after Mendeleev first published his periodic table, the first discovery was made. A French chemist found the first of the missing elements in 1874. It was named gallium. Its atomic weight and physical and chemical properties matched Mendeleev's predictions almost exactly!

In 1878 the element scandium was discovered. It matched another of the blank spots that Mendeleev had left in his periodic table. And in 1886 the third element that Mendeleev had predicted was found. It was named germanium. These discoveries clearly proved that Mendeleev's Periodic Law was correct.

The fourth element that Mendeleev had predicted wasn't found until 1937. It was named technetium, because it was produced in a laboratory. Technetium is radioactive and quickly decays into other elements. It has such a short lifetime that it no longer exists naturally on the Earth. But it does exist. Mendeleev's predictions had all proved true!

The reason *why* the elements follow this periodic pattern was not found until fifty years after Mendeleev's discovery. The laws that describe the structure of atoms, known as quantum mechanics, explain why the elements form groups with similar properties.

Since Mendeleev's time a number of additional elements have been added to the periodic chart. One whole family of elements known as the *inert gases* was discovered in the late 1800s. These gases were difficult to find because they don't react at all with other elements. Helium, argon, neon, krypton, xenon, and radon are all members of this family of elements.

Two other large groups of elements were also discovered. One group is known as the *rare earth elements*. They are found in the Earth's crust only in tiny quantities. The other group is made up of radioactive elements. They are known as *actinides*.

Although all these elements were found after the Periodic Law was discovered, they fit very nicely into the pattern that Mendeleev found. The current periodic table includes 103 elements. They all follow Mendeleev's Periodic Law.

The periodic table today contains 103 elements, all arranged according to their properties.

1	2	3	4	5	6	7	8	9	10	11	12	13	14	15	16	17	18
1 Hydrogen																	2 Helium
3 Lithium	4 Beryllium											5 Boron	6 Carbon	7 Nitrogen	8 Oxygen	9 Fluorine	10 Neon
11 Sodium	12 Magnesium											13 Aluminum	14 Silicon	15 Phosphorus	16 Sulfur	17 Chlorine	18 Argon
19 Potassium	20 Calcium	21 Scandium	22 Titanium	23 Vanadium	24 Chromium	25 Manganese	26 Iron	27 Cobalt	28 Nickel	29 Copper	30 Zinc	31 Gallium	32 Germanium	33 Arsenic	34 Selenium	35 Bromine	36 Krypton
37 Rubidium	38 Strontium	39 Yttrium	40 Zirconium	41 Niobium	42 Molybdenum	43 Technetium	44 Ruthenium	45 Rhodium	46 Palladium	47 Silver	48 Cadmium	49 Indium	50 Tin	51 Antimony	52 Tellurium	53 Iodine	54 Xenon
55 Cesium	56 Barium	see below	72 Hatnium	73 Tantalum	74 Tungsten	75 Rhenium	76 Oxmium	77 Iridium	78 Platinum	79 Gold	80 Mercury	81 Thallium	82 Lead	83 Bismuth	84 Polonium	85 Astatine	86 Radon
87 Francium	88 Radium	see below	104 Rutherfordium	105 Hahnium													

57 Lanthanum	58 Cerium	59 Prasodymium	60 Neodyonium	61 Promethium	62 Samarium	63 Europium	64 Gadolinium	65 Terbium	66 Dysprosium	67 Holmium	68 Erbium	69 Thulium	70 Ytterbium	71 Lutetium
89 Actinium	90 Therium	91 Protactinium	92 Uranium	93 Neptunium	94 Plutonium	95 Americium	96 Curium	97 Berkelium	98 Californium	99 Einsteinium	100 Fermium	101 Mendelevium	102 Nobelium	103 Lawrencium

15.

THE FIRST LAW OF THERMODYNAMICS— CONSERVATION OF ENERGY

Every time we lift an object, move it, push it, or carry it, we are doing work. And each time we do work, we use energy, or force. If we use our muscles, that energy comes from the food we eat. If we use a machine, the energy comes from oil, gasoline, coal, electricity, or some other energy source. Even a tree needs energy to lift its water and minerals high above the ground. The energy for that work comes from the sun.

Without energy no work can be done. In fact, scientists define *energy* as the ability to do work. But what happens to energy after its work is completed? Is it "used up"? Does it disappear or just return to where it came from? Does it become a part of the object it was used on, or does it change into something else?

Scientists have discovered that energy is *conserved*. Energy may change forms, but it is neither created nor destroyed. That rule is known as the Law of Conservation of Energy.

Discovering this law wasn't the work of a single researcher. Many famous scientists contributed to the understanding of heat and the other forms of energy. Several different scientists have been given credit for first discovering the law itself. One of the two most often named is the English scientist James Prescott Joule. His experiments about energy transformations were published in 1843. The German scientist Hermann von

Helmholtz is credited with writing the law in its final form in 1847.

The story of the Law of Conservation of Energy begins with Christiaan Huygens in the late 1600s. He is the same Dutch scientist who invented the pendulum clock. Huygens wondered what happened to the energy of moving objects when they collided. He imagined what would happen when perfectly hard billiard balls bumped into one another. He realized that the force of one ball would be transferred to the other balls as it hit them.

In the game of pool, a player is allowed to hit only the white cue ball. The cue ball then hits other balls, transferring its energy to them. The motion of the cue ball is transferred to the ball it hits. If the player has aimed correctly, the transferred

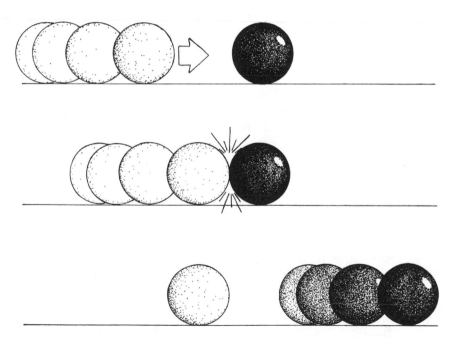

A moving cue ball transfers its kinetic energy to a second ball as it strikes it.

energy will send the other ball exactly where he wants it to go.

The energy of motion is called *kinetic energy*. Huygens concluded that kinetic energy could be transferred completely from one ball to another *if* the two balls were perfectly hard. The total amount of energy would be conserved. That means no energy would be lost in the transfer.

Of course, there is no such thing as a perfectly hard ball. When real balls collide, kinetic energy is not completely transferred from one ball to the other. Some energy is lost to friction. Some is absorbed by the balls themselves as they are temporarily dented when they collide. Some straight-line motion may be converted into spinning motion.

It wasn't until the middle of the 1800s that scientists were finally sure that the total amount of energy in any action stays the same. None of the energy is really "lost." It just changes forms. It may be changed from the energy of motion to heat or from heat to light or from electricity to motion. But no new energy is created, and none is lost. That is what the Law of Conservation of Energy says: Energy may change forms, but it can neither be created nor destroyed.

Energy comes in several different forms. It can take the form of heat, light, electricity, mechanical energy (movement), chemical energy (like the energy in coal, gasoline, or food), or nuclear energy. The Law of Conservation of Energy tells us that energy can be converted from any of these forms to any other form. It is still energy, and none of it disappears when it is converted.

In the 1700s scientists were not sure that heat was a kind of energy. Most thought that heat was a weightless, invisible fluid, which they called *caloric*. However, in 1798 Count Rumford proved that caloric doesn't exist and that heat is just another form of energy.

Rumford studied the heat produced when cannon barrels were drilled out. The more drilling that was done, the more heat that was produced. The metal never seemed to run out of heat as it was drilled. Rumford measured the heat and proved

that it couldn't have all come from the caloric in the little pile
of metal shavings that the drilling produced. Instead, it had
to be produced by the friction created as the drill spun around
in the cannon. Rumford's experiment proved that heat is not
a substance after all. It is a form of energy.

In the early 1800s James Prescott Joule began studying how
the energy of motion changes into heat. Joule and his fellow
scientists lived at a time when steam engines were being used
in many industries. Wherever he looked, Joule could see examples of energy being converted from one form to another. Steam
engines got their energy by burning coal, a source of chemical
energy. The engines turned the chemical energy into the motion
of pistons, wheels, and pulleys. That energy was then used to
do work of many different kinds. Steam engines could even
generate electrical energy. Joule realized that any form of energy
can be transformed into any other form.

You can easily transform chemical energy to mechanical energy to heat energy using nothing but your own two hands.
Put the palms of your hands together and rub them vigorously

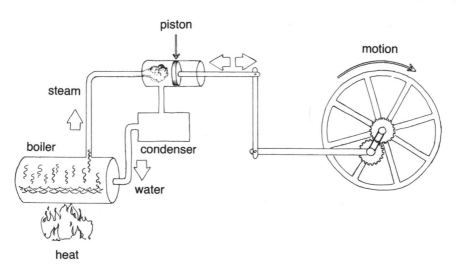

*A steam engine changes the heat energy of boiling water to mechanical
energy, which is then used to do work.*

for thirty seconds. You will feel quite a bit of heat. Your muscles transform the chemical energy of the food you eat into motion. The friction between your two hands transforms their kinetic energy into heat.

A similar thing happens when you hammer a nail. Try hammering a large nail most of the way into a block of wood. Then feel the head of the nail. It will be warm. Some of the energy of your hammering has pushed the nail into the wood, and some of it has turned into heat energy, warming the nail, the wood, and even the air around you.

One way to start a fire is to focus the sun's rays on a pile of dry tinder with a magnifying glass. In this case, light energy is converted into enough heat energy to start a fire.

Joule designed a series of clever experiments to show that when energy changes form, none of it disappears. In his most famous experiment, he attached a weight on a cable to a paddle wheel. The paddle wheel turned in a container of water. The falling weight turned the paddle wheel. Joule knew exactly how much energy the weight used as it fell. As the paddle wheel turned, its motion heated the water. Joule carefully measured the change in water temperature. The amount of extra heat in the water equaled the energy of the falling weight exactly. The form of the energy was changed from motion to heat, but no energy was lost.

Because Joule and his fellow researchers concentrated on studying the movement of heat energy, the branch of physics they were studying is called *thermodynamics*. The prefix *thermo-* means *heat,* and *dynamics* is the study of motion. The Law of Conservation of Energy is also known as the First Law of Thermodynamics.

Because of James Prescott Joule's contributions to the study of energy, the metric unit used to measure work is named in his honor.

Machines do work by converting one form of energy to another. For example, a car converts the chemical energy in gaso-

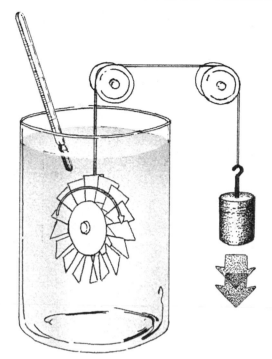

As the weight falls, the paddle wheel turns and the temperature of the water rises.

line to kinetic energy (motion). The Law of Conservation of Energy tells us that a machine *must* have a source of energy. It cannot create its own. And a machine cannot supply more power than it gets from its energy source. When the energy runs out, the machine stops.

The same rule is true for living things. Plants get the power they need to live and grow from the sun's energy. Without that energy supply, plants will die. They cannot produce their own energy. Animals must eat food to supply themselves with energy for life. They too will die when their energy supply runs out.

Energy can neither be created nor destroyed. So the energy of any system, machine or creature must balance out in the end. No energy can be lost or gained. That means it is possible to trace the energy "budget" of any object to see where the energy comes from and where it goes.

When a person goes on a diet, he uses the Law of Conservation of Energy to change his personal energy budget. When a person eats, he takes in chemical energy in the form of food. The amount of energy he takes in is measured in calories. Those calories are then converted to energy for walking, running, talking, thinking, and so on. They also are converted to heat as the body does its work. The more food a person takes in, the more energy he must convert to keep his energy budget balanced. If a person takes in more energy than he can use, the extra gets stored as fat.

A dieter eats less, and so he takes in less food energy. If he keeps up a normal level of activity, he will get the remaining

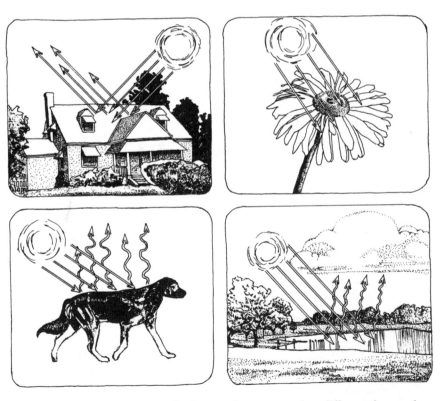

Sunlight striking the Earth changes into many other different forms of energy.

energy he needs by burning the fat stored in his body. As the fat is converted to energy, the dieter loses weight.

Even the Earth as a whole has its own "energy budget." The Earth receives almost all of its energy from the sun in the form of light. Some of that energy reflects back into space. Some turns into heat, which warms the Earth. The Earth later radiates that heat back into space. Some solar energy is captured by plants and is turned into chemical energy by their leaves. Some sunlight provides energy to evaporate water, form clouds, and produce rain. But the totals all balance out. The Law of Conservation of Energy tells us that no matter what we do, we cannot end up with more energy than we started with—or less.

The same law holds true for the whole universe. The universe has a certain total amount of energy. The total energy of the universe is enormous, of course. There are billions of stars burning with vast storehouses of energy. But the energy in the universe is *not* limitless. No new energy is being created anywhere in the universe, and none is being lost. It is just endlessly changing its forms.

16.

THE SECOND LAW OF THERMODYNAMICS— ENTROPY

Thermodynamics is the science of energy transformations. In the last chapter we learned about the First Law of Thermodynamics. It tells us that energy cannot be created or destroyed, but it can be transformed. The Second Law of Thermodynamics tells us what happens in those transformations.

Here's an experiment to try: Fill a coffee cup with hot water. Measure its temperature. Then place it on a table and leave it there for two hours. When you return, check the temperature again. It will be much cooler, of course. We know that the heat energy in that hot water couldn't just disappear. The First Law of Thermodynamics tells us that. So where did that energy go?

It is in the air of the room. The heat of the water was gradually transferred to the molecules in the surrounding air. If you had a very sensitive thermometer, you could even measure the slight rise in air temperature that resulted from the heat transfer. The energy of that hot water still exists, but it has spread out into the room.

Now try to put that energy back into the cup of water. Collect the spread-out heat energy from the air and bring the water in the cup back to its original temperature.

It can't be done! The energy still exists, but to collect it and put it back in a concentrated form is impossible. At least it is impossible without using lots *more* energy to collect it.

That impossible experiment is an example of the Second Law of Thermodynamics. The scientists who first stated the Second Law of Thermodynamics were Rudolf Clausius of Germany and William Thomson, Lord Kelvin, of England. However, many others also contributed to the understanding of this law, which was first published in 1850.

There are several different ways of stating the Second Law of Thermodynamics. One way of saying it is this: In any energy transformation, heat always flows from areas of higher concentration to areas of lower concentration.

That means that heat always moves from hotter areas to cooler ones. The heat energy in any system has a tendency to "spread out" until finally everything is the same temperature.

To see this law in action, you will need a glass and a small pitcher, hot and cold water, some red food coloring, and a large spoon. Fill the glass half full of cold water. Pour a few

Pouring hot water gently over the cold water creates two temperature layers.

ounces of very hot water into the pitcher, and then color it with six or eight drops of the red dye. The red dye will show where the heat is concentrated in the water. The clear water represents the area of less heat.

Place the spoon just at the surface of the cold water in the glass. Now gently pour the hot water onto the spoon. If you pour slowly and carefully, the hot water will form a separate layer on top of the cold water.

As time passes, the red-hot water gradually mixes with the cold water. After a while, the dye will be completely mixed into pale pink water. Along with the dye, the heat in the water will be spread evenly throughout the glass.

Another way of saying the same law is: In any energy transformation some useful energy will be lost and turned into unrecoverable heat.

Heat is the least useful form that energy can take. The Second Law of Thermodynamics tells us that whenever energy is put to use, some of it will be turned into *waste heat*. Waste heat is energy that can no longer do useful work. The word for this loss of useful, organized energy is *entropy*. The Second Law of Thermodynamics is also known as the Law of Entropy.

The Law of Entropy means that energy transformations are *not reversible*. You can't reassemble a piece of firewood after it has been burned. The Laws of Conservation of Matter and Energy tell us that all the energy and material still exist. But they have spread out. You can't collect all that matter and energy and put the log back together again. It's like trying to unscramble an egg and put it back in the shell. It can't be done.

Consider what happens when you run a lawnmower. The lawnmower gets its power from the chemical energy in gasoline. As the gasoline burns in the engine, it is converted to mechanical energy. The blades and wheels of the mower turn, doing useful work. But not all of the energy from the gasoline is turned into useful work. Most of it is turned into heat. Heat escapes into the air with the hot exhaust gases. More heat radiates into the air from the hot engine. All that heat is "wasted" energy. It does no useful work. It just spreads out into the air, making the air slightly warmer. It still exists, but nothing more can be done with it.

The same thing always happens when machines use energy. No machine can be perfectly efficient. That means no machine can use 100 percent of its energy to do work. Some energy always leaks away as heat.

This fact was first discovered by the French engineer Sadi Carnot. He was trying to calculate just how efficient the perfect steam engine could be. Steam engines produce power when hot steam pushes against pistons. To keep the power coming, this motion must be repeated over and over again. But that means the same steam can't remain in the piston's cylinder. The "used" steam must be removed, to allow the engine to recycle for another burst of power. The exhaust steam must then be cooled back into water and returned to the boiler to produce more steam.

Carnot realized that in order to work, the steam engine *must* lose some heat as the steam cools. It also loses energy as heat

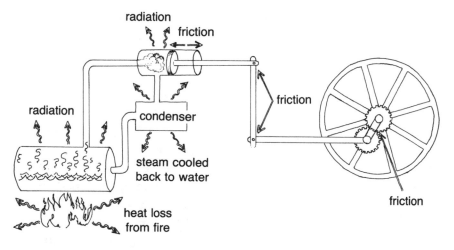

Most of the heat energy in a steam engine is wasted. Only a small fraction of it is converted to useful work.

"leaks" from the hotter portions of the machinery to the cooler ones. It loses more heat as smoke from the burning coal escapes up the chimney. It loses still more heat as the parts of the machinery rub against each other, producing friction. Even under perfect conditions, most of the energy of the burning coal is lost as waste heat.

We can see examples of entropy, or the loss of useful energy, wherever energy is used. For example, a lamp wastes part of its electrical energy by producing heat as well as light. If you put your hand near a lightbulb, you can feel it. Household appliances, like blenders, vacuum cleaners, washing machines, and refrigerators, also produce heat as they work. Automobiles produce useless heat in their exhaust and in the friction of their moving parts. Even a baseball thrown through the air loses some of its energy to the heat of friction as it rubs against the molecules of the air.

Living creatures are also subject to the Law of Entropy. Muscles produce heat as they work. Anyone who has ever run a race knows that. After you run, you're hot. As you cool off, the heat gradually spreads out into the air around you.

Your body's energy comes from food. But you cannot convert anywhere near 100 percent of that food energy into useful activity. Most of it becomes body heat, much of which is lost to the air around you.

The Laws of Thermodynamics prove that a "perpetual motion" machine can never be built. For hundreds of years people have tried to design a machine that could run forever under its own power. Unfortunately, it is completely hopeless. There is no way that any machine can produce the energy to keep itself running, much less create additional energy to do useful work. The First Law of Thermodynamics tells us that energy cannot be created. And the Second Law of Thermodynamics tells us that every machine *must* lose energy as it works. You simply can't win when you turn energy into work. So a machine that would provide its own power to keep running forever is impossible.

The Law of Entropy has another interesting and even scary result. It tells us that the universe is slowly running down! Every time there is a transformation of energy, energy spreads out and becomes less concentrated. This happens in the collisions of planets, nuclear reactions in the stars, chemical reactions between atoms, the friction of two gears rubbing together, and all the other events happening throughout the universe.

The Law of Entropy tells us that all energy in the universe will eventually level out. Everything in the universe will be at the same temperature. No more energy transformations will be possible, and all activity in the universe will come to a stop. This final state is sometimes called the *heat death* of the universe.

That idea does sound frightening. However, we don't really need to worry about it. The universe is still full of usable energy, and so the end won't come for billions of years. In fact, scientists still don't know whether this heat death will happen at all. It depends on how much matter there is in the entire universe.

The universe is still expanding. But if there is enough matter in the universe, gravitational force will take over eventually. The expansion of the universe will slow, stop, and then reverse. After billions of years, gravity will pull all the mass of the universe back together again to one tiny point. Then there will be another Big Bang, and the universe will start all over again. If that is true, then the universe expands and contracts over and over again. That would mean that the energy of the universe would recharge itself, and the heat death predicted by the Law of Entropy would never happen.

But perhaps there is *not* enough mass in the universe to stop its expansion with gravitational force. If that is the case, then the creation of the universe is a one-time event. The universe will continue expanding and cooling and the Law of Entropy will continue in effect. The energy level of the universe will continue to run down until, billions of years from now, the universe will be evenly cold and lifeless everywhere.

It's still a mystery! No one knows yet which possibility is correct. Scientists do not yet know how much matter there is in the universe. Perhaps scientists will discover another possible fate for our universe. But meanwhile the Law of Entropy is in effect. Little by little, every event turns some of the universe's useful energy into useless heat.

17.

LAWS OF ELECTROMAGNETISM

In the late 1700s electricity was a popular amusement at parties. Guests would collect electrical charges using glass rods and scraps of silk. Then they would shock each other with electric sparks, make their hair stand on end, and do other electrical parlor tricks. Electricity was a fascinating toy. But it also was a puzzle to the scientists who were trying to study it seriously.

The most popular theory of electricity at that time said that electricity was made of two fluids. One fluid had a positive charge, and one was negative. There were many ways of collecting these "fluids." For example, rubbing a glass rod with fur transferred some of the fluids, creating an electrical charge. The opposite fluids would then attract each other. But no one had seen electrical fluids or found any other evidence that they really existed.

No single scientist was responsible for discovering all the principles that describe electrical forces. James Clerk Maxwell was the scientist who finally wrote the complete set of laws for the workings of electricity and magnetism. But the mathematical laws that Maxwell published in 1864 were the result of many years of work by many different scientists.

Let's begin the story with Benjamin Franklin. You probably know Franklin as a great American statesman, writer, and inventor. But he was also an early investigator of electricity. Franklin realized that electricity could be explained just as easily with one fluid as with two. Positive charge could be considered an extra amount of the fluid. Negative charge would then be a shortage of the same substance. The fluid theory didn't last, but Franklin's idea of positive and negative charges being two sides of a single force did.

Franklin also recognized a very important law of electricity: the Law of Conservation of Charge. The Law of Conservation of Charge says that for every negative charge created, there must be an equal amount of positive charge. That means that the total of all positive and negative charges in the universe must balance each other perfectly.

The Law of Conservation of Charge doesn't mean that we can't have any electricity. But whenever we unbalance electrical forces, we must create positive and negative charges in equal amounts. You can create an electrical charge by rubbing an inflated balloon against a wool sweater. The balloon will pick up a slight negative charge from the wool. But the wool will also receive an equal amount of positive charge. The balloon will then stick to a wall because of the difference in electrical charge between the wall and the balloon.

The same thing happens when we shuffle our feet across a rug on a dry day. As we walk across the rug, our body picks up a small electrical charge. An equal amount of opposite charge is built up in the rug. When you touch a doorknob or other metal object, the charges cancel out with a tiny spark. If you do this in a dark room, you will be able to see the spark clearly.

It's important to remember that whenever we give one object a negative charge, we give the other object a positive charge at the same time. The wool gets just as much positive charge as the balloon gets a negative charge. Each object receives a charge, and the charges balance each other. That is the Law of Conservation of Charge.

The next discovery of electrical law was made by the French scientist Charles de Coulomb in 1789. Coulomb knew that opposite electrical forces attract each other and like forces repel each other. He wanted to measure the strength of that attraction.

To measure electrical force, Coulomb used a device very similar to the instrument Cavendish used to measure the force of gravity (see page 49). He suspended a rod from a thin wire. At each end of the rod was an electrically charged ball made of a corklike material. He then gave an opposite charge to two other balls nearby. He knew exactly how much charge each ball had. By measuring the amount of twist in the wire, he could calculate the force of attraction between the balls.

Coulomb's results were surprising and exciting. He discovered that electrical force is directly proportional to the amount of charge in the two objects and inversely proportional to the square of their distance.

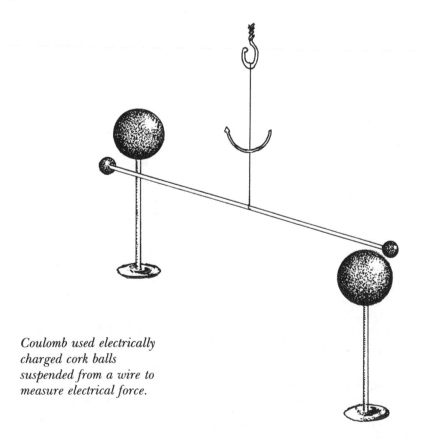

Coulomb used electrically
charged cork balls
suspended from a wire to
measure electrical force.

Coulomb's Law tells us that the electrical force between two charges depends on the strength of the two charges. The larger the difference in the electrical charges between two objects, the stronger the attraction between them. It also means that as two objects get farther apart, the attraction decreases rapidly. If two objects are moved twice as far apart, the attraction is only one-fourth as much. If they are moved three times as far apart, the force is only one-ninth as much.

Mathematically, Coulomb's Law is written like this:

$$F = K \times \frac{q(1) \times q(2)}{d^2}$$

In this equation *F* stands for the force of attraction, *q(1)* and *q(2)* are the charges of the two objects, and *d* is the distance between the objects. *K* is a constant, a small number that allows the amount of attraction to be calculated precisely.

Does Coulomb's Law look or sound familiar? It is the same inverse square relationship as Newton's Law of Universal Gravitation. Go back to page 44 and look at Newton's law. The mathematical forms of the two laws look almost identical! Coulomb had discovered that gravitation and electrical force work in very similar ways.

Coulomb also experimented with magnetic force in the same way. It turned out that the law of magnetic attraction was also an inverse square law. It was very exciting to discover that these different forces all follow similar laws. It showed that the laws of the universe must fit into a simple and orderly pattern.

The next important discovery about electricity was made by Hans Christian Oersted in 1820. Oersted made his discovery by accident. He connected a wire to a battery to make an electric circuit. A magnetic compass happened to be sitting on the laboratory table nearby. Oersted noticed that when electricity was flowing through the wire, the compass needle was attracted to it.

After more experimenting, Oersted was sure of his discovery: A moving electrical charge creates magnetic force. Whenever an electric current flows through a wire, it creates magnetic forces around the wire.

You can do Oersted's experiment yourself. All you will need is a length of insulated wire, a small magnetic compass, and a battery. Use a 1.5-volt dry cell or a 6-volt flashlight battery.

Strip a small amount of insulation off each end of the wire. Attach one end of the wire to one terminal of the battery. Form the wire into a loop and place the compass near the loop of wire. Arrange the wire in such a way that the compass needle is not pointing directly toward the wire. Now touch the other end of the wire to the other pole of the battery.

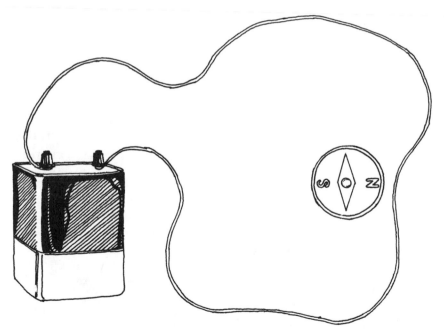

An electric current flowing in a wire creates magnetic forces, as this simple experiment shows.

Watch how the compass responds. Try the experiment with the compass and wire in several different positions. Don't leave the wire connected to both poles of the battery for more than a few seconds at a time. The completed circuit will quickly drain the energy out of the battery and could make the wire dangerously hot.

After 1820 the study of electricity and magnetism moved at a very rapid rate. Oersted had found that electricity could exert enough force to make a magnetic needle spin in a compass. Stronger electric currents and stronger magnets could be combined to spin a motor. Using Oersted's discovery, the first electromagnet and the first electric motor were both built in 1823.

The English scientist Michael Faraday made the next major contribution to the understanding of electricity and magnets. Faraday was a brilliant experimenter. He knew from Oersted's experiment that a moving current could create magnetic force. He wondered if the opposite was also true. Could a magnet cause an electric current to flow in a wire?

His answer has turned out to be one of the most useful discoveries in the history of science. In 1831 Faraday made a circuit with a coil of wire. In the circuit was a galvanometer, an instrument that measures small amounts of electric current. Faraday then put a magnet inside the coil. He discovered that a current was created in the wire whenever the magnet was moved in or out of the coil. When the magnet was just sitting still, no electricity flowed.

From this experiment came what is known as Faraday's Law: A moving magnetic field creates an electric current in a wire.

Why was Faraday's discovery so useful? Faraday quickly realized that moving a wire through a powerful magnetic field could generate an electric current. That same year he built the first electromagnetic generator. Faraday's generator could produce a steady supply of electricity whenever it was needed. Faraday's invention didn't depend on expensive, messy supplies of chemicals as batteries did. And it never ran out of power.

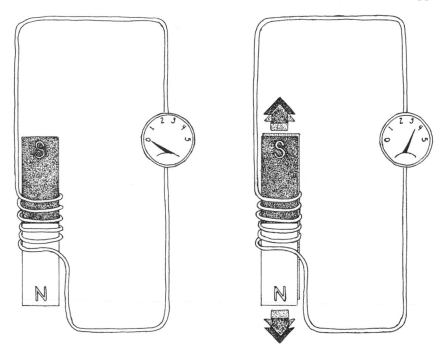

Faraday proved that a moving magnet creates an electric current in a wire.

Today huge descendants of Faraday's first generator produce the electricity for our TVs, refrigerators, electric lights, and all our many other electrical appliances.

In 1864 James Clerk Maxwell took all the pieces of the electricity and magnetism puzzle and put them together. His mathematical laws of electromagnetism are known as Maxwell's Equations. The mathematical statements of the laws are too complicated to go into here, but his laws tell us the following things:

- Electricity and magnetism are two different aspects of the *same* force.
- Every electrical charge has an electrical field around it. This field attracts opposite charges and repels like charges.

· A moving electrical charge or field generates a magnetic field.
· A moving magnetic field generates an electrical field.

Since 1864 experiments have shown Maxwell's laws to be correct again and again. Because magnetism and electricity are just different aspects of the same force, scientists usually refer to that force as *electromagnetic force*. Along with gravitation and the nuclear forces in atoms, it is one of the basic forces of the universe.

As Maxwell considered his discovery, he realized something else very interesting. A change in an electric field creates a change in a magnetic field. But a change in a magnetic field then creates a change in an electric field. This process can continue on and on. So a single change in an electric or magnetic field spreads out very rapidly, creating an electromagnetic wave effect.

Maxwell calculated how quickly this wave would move through space. His results said that it would travel at 300,000 kilometers per second. But that is a well-known speed. It is the speed of light. Could it be that light is a form of electromagnetic energy?

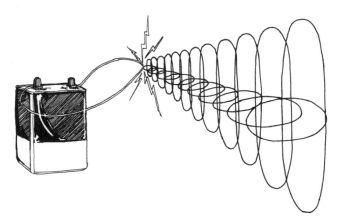

Maxwell discovered that a changing electric field creates a series of electromagnetic waves that travel at the speed of light.

Yes. Maxwell discovered that light is an electromagnetic wave. More recent discoveries have shown that light radiation is actually generated by the rapid vibration of electrons in atoms.

Maxwell also predicted that researchers would find other kinds of electromagnetic radiation besides visible light. Maxwell's equations said there should be "light" waves with lower amounts of energy than visible light, and "light" waves with higher amounts of energy.

Two of these other kinds of light waves were already known. Infrared and ultraviolet light had both been discovered around 1800. Maxwell's calculations showed that these light waves are forms of electromagnetic radiation, just as visible light is. And it wasn't long after Maxwell's laws were published that other new forms of electromagnetic radiation were discovered.

In 1889 Heinrich Hertz discovered the existence of radio waves. These are electromagnetic waves with much longer wavelengths than visible light. In 1895 Wilhelm Roentgen discovered X-rays. These are "light" waves with very short wavelengths. The wide range of radiation—from radio waves, through infrared waves, visible light, ultraviolet light, and powerful X-rays and gamma rays—is known as the *electromagnetic spectrum*. All these different rays travel at 300,000 kilometers per second. They all behave as visible light does. Maxwell's predictions about electromagnetic energy were proved true!

In 1897 J. J. Thomson discovered the existence of a negatively charged particle smaller than an atom. This particle became known as the electron. Scientists realized that it is the motion of electrons that carries electrical energy.

When a balloon is rubbed against wool, some electrons are transferred from the wool fibers to the rubber. It is that transfer that creates the electrical charge. When we connect a wire to both terminals of a battery, it is the flow of electrons that creates an electric current. And when we turn on a lamp, it is the vibration of electrons in the filament of the lightbulb that creates the electromagnetic waves we call light.

It's hard to imagine what life today would be like without electric power. Understanding electromagnetic force has made many amazing devices possible. We use this force to run our appliances, heat and light our homes, and calculate our household budgets. Computers, television, tape recorders, radar, and a thousand other miraculous devices depend on our understanding of electromagnetism.

18.

ELECTRIC CURRENT—OHM'S LAW AND JOULE'S LAW

Electricity has become the most widely used form of energy in our modern world. But to put electricity to use, we must know how it acts in a circuit. With that knowledge, electrical appliances and equipment can be designed to work safely and efficiently.

In the 1800s electricity was thought of as a flow of electrical charges through any conductor, such as a wire. We now know that those electrical charges are tiny particles called electrons. Electrical energy is actually produced by the movement of electrons in the circuit.

A circuit is the path through which electrical current flows. It is usually a series of wires and electrical devices connected to a source of electrical energy.

The electrical energy in a circuit is generated by a power source. This source can be a battery, which makes electrical energy by chemical reaction. Or it can be a generator, or *dynamo,* which produces electricity by moving wires through a magnetic field. Commercial power companies generate electricity with huge dynamos powered by water power, coal or oil furnaces, or nuclear reactors.

The power source, either generator or battery, creates an *electromotive force.* You can think of electromotive force as the amount of electrical "pressure" that sends the current around the circuit. The electromotive force in a circuit is measured in volts (named in honor of Alessandro Volta, the inventor of the battery).

The electromotive force is often called a *potential difference*, or just *potential*. It produces an electric current only when a circuit connecting the positive and negative poles of the power source is completed. Otherwise, it just has the *potential*, or possibility, of creating a flow of current. A 6-volt battery has 6 volts of electrical potential whether it is connected to a circuit or not.

The amount of electrical charge flowing through a circuit is called the *current*. It is measured in amperes (named for André Ampère, another electrical scientist). Amperes measure the number of electrons flowing through the circuit per second.

Remember that current and voltage are two different things. It is possible to have a large amount of current flowing through a circuit at a low voltage or a little bit of current flowing at a very high voltage. Voltage measures the electric *force*, and amperage measures the total *amount* of electricity that is flowing in a circuit.

As electricity flows around a circuit, it meets with resistance. Resistance is anything that restricts or opposes the flow of electricity in a circuit. Resistance in a circuit turns some of the electrical energy into heat. Electrical resistance is measured in ohms (named for Georg Ohm, whom we will learn more about shortly).

Everything in an electrical circuit, including the wires, develops some resistance. The amount of resistance in a circuit depends on four things: the length of the circuit, the thickness of the wires and other conductors in the circuit, the kind of material the wire is made of, and its temperature.

Some wires, like those made of silver or copper, have very little resistance. They conduct electricity quite well. Very little of the electrical energy passing through copper wire is turned into heat by resistance. That's why copper is often used for electric circuits. Others have more resistance. For example, Nichrome wire, which is made from a combination of nickel and chromium, has a lot of resistance. It gets very hot when a current passes through it. Nichrome is used for the heating elements in toasters and hair dryers for this reason.

Some materials like glass and rubber have so much resistance that electricity won't flow through them at all. Materials like these are used as insulators.

The longer a piece of wire is, the more resistance it has. And the thicker a wire is, the *less* resistance it has. Like water flowing through a large pipe, electricity flows more easily through a thick conductor.

The temperature of a material also affects its resistance. In most cases, electrical resistance increases as the temperature increases. But there are exceptions to this rule.

To help you understand the movement of electricity in a circuit, picture the similarities between an electric circuit and a system of water pipes. In a water system, the water is forced through the pipes by a pump. The pump corresponds to the generator or battery in an electrical circuit. The pump creates pressure, which forces the water through the system. That corresponds to the electromotive force, or voltage. The amount of water flowing through the pipes corresponds to the amount of current in a circuit.

Resistance is similar to the friction in the pipes of a water system. The pump must push against this friction to move the water. Like friction, resistance in an electric circuit generates heat. Large pipes allow water to flow more easily, while small pipes have much more friction to restrict the flow. Thicker wires also have less resistance to electrical flow than thin wires.

In the early 1800s the German physicist Georg Ohm investigated the workings of electrical circuits. He wanted to know how resistance and voltage affect the flow of electric current in a wire. Ohm found that when he increased the voltage in a circuit, the amount of current also increased, as long as everything else in the circuit stayed the same. Suppose we had a 10-volt circuit with 1 ampere of current flowing through it. If

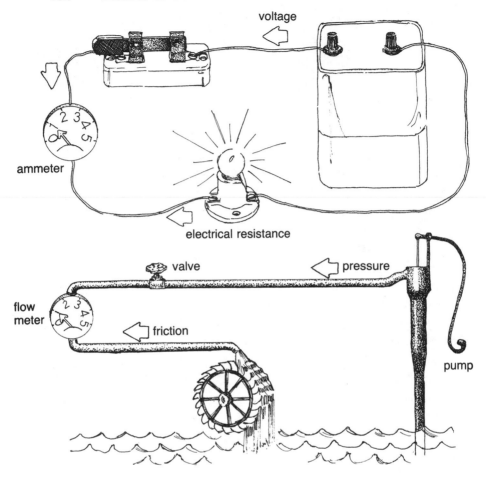

An electrical circuit has many similarities to a circular water system.

we doubled the voltage of the circuit to 20 volts, we also would double the amount of current to 2 amps.

Ohm also discovered that the amount of current flowing through a circuit *decreased* when he increased the amount of resistance in the circuit. If we made the wire in our 10-volt circuit twice as long, that would create twice as much resistance. As a result, only half an ampere of current would flow through the circuit.

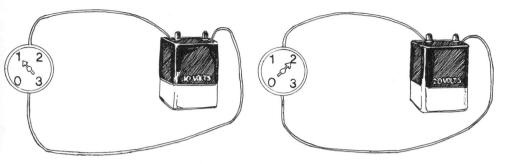

If you increase the voltage in a circuit, the amount of current also increases, if everything else remains unchanged.

In 1826 Ohm published his findings. These discoveries are now known as Ohm's Law. Ohm's Law is stated like this: The flow of current in a circuit is directly proportional to the electromotive force (voltage) and inversely proportional to resistance.

Think about our comparison between electricity and water flow one more time. The amount of water flowing through a

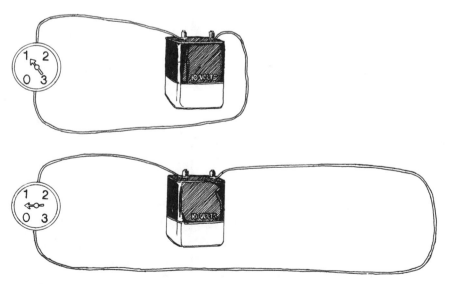

If you increase the resistance in a circuit, the amount of current decreases, if everything else remains unchanged.

pipe depends on the pressure of the water and the size of the pipe. If the pump increases the pressure (higher pressure equals higher voltage), more water will flow through the pipe. If the pipe is made thinner (thinner pipe equals more resistance), less water will flow through it. Ohm's Law tells us that something very similar happens with electricity. The amount of electricity flowing in a circuit depends on the voltage (electric "pressure") and the resistance of the circuit.

Mathematically, Ohm's Law is written like this:

$$\text{current} = \frac{\text{voltage}}{\text{resistance}} \quad or \quad I = \frac{E}{R}$$

In this equation I stands for the intensity or amount of current in amperes. E stands for the electromotive force or voltage of the circuit, and R stands for the resistance.

Notice that the amount of current (I) is expressed as a fraction. If we increase the voltage (E), the numerator of the fraction gets larger. So the value of the fraction as a whole is larger. More voltage in the circuit results in more current.

But when we increase the resistance (R), the denominator of the fraction becomes larger. That makes the value of the fraction smaller. More resistance in the circuit results in less current.

Ohm's Law tells us that when there is a lot of resistance, less current will flow. If there is less resistance, more current will flow. That explains why people receive the most dangerous electric shocks when their skin is wet.

Dry skin is not a good conductor. It has lots of resistance. So when a person with dry skin accidentally touches electrical wires and completes a circuit, not much current can flow through his body. That small amount of current does little harm. But if a person is damp, especially if he is touching a good conductor like water or metal, his electrical resistance is much less. He becomes a much better conductor, and so more current can flow through his body, causing a dangerous shock.

A few years after Georg Ohm made his discovery, the English physicist James Joule made his own investigation of how electrical energy works. Joule was interested in how one form of energy can be converted to another. One of the changes he studied was the conversion of electric energy to heat.

Power is the amount of energy delivered in each unit of time. Electric power is measured in watts (named in honor of James Watt, inventor of the steam engine). Joule measured the power that electric circuits deliver by seeing how much heat they could generate in a certain amount of time. In fact, much of the electric power in our homes is used the same way—for heat to keep us warm or to cook our food.

Joule found that the amount of power in an electric circuit depends on two things: the voltage of the circuit and the amount of current flowing in it. The more current a circuit has, the more power it delivers. And the more voltage a circuit has, the more power it delivers. The heat (power) produced by a circuit can be calculated by multiplying the voltage times the amount of current:

Heat (power) = Voltage × Current   *or*   H = E × I

This rule is known as Joule's Law. Joule's Law tells us that increasing either the current or the voltage in a circuit increases the power that the circuit produces.

All the electrical appliances we plug into our household circuits use electrical energy to do work. They transform the electrical energy into heat, light, or motion. The appliances all add more resistance in the circuits. It is the resistance in the wires of an oven that generates the heat to bake our bread or roast our chicken for dinner. This intentional resistance in a circuit is called the *load*.

The electric motors in our blenders, washing machines, and vacuum cleaners all have electrical resistance. They place an increased load on the circuit as they are running. If you place your hand near the electric motor of any appliance, you will be able to feel the heat that its electrical resistance generates. In ordinary house current the *voltage* always stays about the same—110 volts. But the electric company will supply us with as much *current* as we can use. So when we need more power to run our home appliances, the amount of current in the circuits increases. In our homes, when we use more power, we have more amperes flowing through our circuits.

Joule's Law explains why an electric oven is more expensive to use than a toaster. An electric oven needs to produce much more heat than a little toaster does. So ovens use a lot more current than toasters. More current flowing through an appliance generates more power, or more heat. But we have to buy that power from the electric company. The more power we use, the more we have to pay.

Joule's Law also explains why we use fuses or circuit breakers in the electric circuits in our home. When we overload a circuit with too many appliances, the wires must carry a large amount of current. Wires all have some resistance to the flow of electricity, and resistance generates heat. The more current that is

As we use more lights and appliances, the amount of current flowing in our home's electrical circuits increases.

flowing in the wires, the more heat that is produced. If the wires get too hot, they can easily start a fire.

A "short circuit" occurs when the two wires in a circuit touch without an appliance in the circuit. That can happen if the insulation on the wires melts or gets worn. Without the resistance of an appliance in the circuit, a large amount of current will flow through the wires easily. All that current can also create enough heat in the wires to start a fire.

Fortunately, every household circuit also has a fuse or circuit breaker in it. Fuses act just like any other piece of wire in a circuit. They conduct electricity as part of the circuit, and they

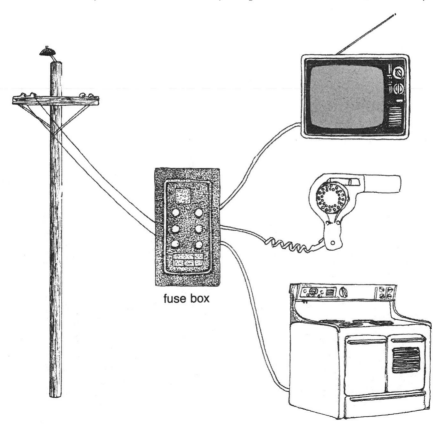

fuse box

Fuses or circuit breakers prevent too much current from flowing through the circuits in our home.

also have some resistance. They get hotter and hotter as more current flows through them. But fuses are designed to melt when too much current passes through them. When a fuse melts, it breaks the electric circuit. No more current can flow. That puts an end to the electrical overload that might otherwise get hot enough to cause a fire. Circuit breakers perform the same safety function, but they don't have to be replaced each time they "blow."

Every time you turn on a light or make a piece of toast or iron a shirt, the discoveries of Georg Ohm, James Joule, and their fellow researchers are working for you. Understanding Ohm's Law, Joule's Law, and the other laws of circuits allows electricians and electrical engineers to make our electrified world safe and efficient.

19.

RELATIVITY

Picture yourself riding down the road in your family's car. The speedometer says that you are traveling 50 miles per hour. But how fast are you *really* going?

If you look out the window, you'll see the countryside moving past you at 50 miles per hour. But if you look at the person sitting next to you in the car, it looks as if he or she isn't moving at all. You're both sitting perfectly still. Are you really moving or not?

If you think about the situation further, it gets even more puzzling. Your car is traveling on the surface of the Earth. The Earth is rotating on its axis at about 1,000 miles per hour, and so is everything on it. Perhaps you are really moving *that* fast.

But wait. The entire Earth is traveling around the sun at a speed of 18 miles per second. And the solar system is moving through our galaxy at a speed of about 150 miles per second. Which is the correct speed for your car?

The answer is: It depends on what you're comparing your speed to. You can't measure speed unless you choose something else to measure it against. Your car's speedometer measures your speed by comparing it to the road, which it considers to be standing still.

Suppose you toss a ball up and down as you sit in your car riding down the road. You would see the ball going straight up and down. But someone standing by the roadside watching you drive by would see something completely different. He/she would see the ball moving forward as it goes up and down. Both of you would be correct, from your own points of view. What the ball is *really* doing depends on how it is being seen.

The name for this idea is *relativity*. Relativity means that what you observe and measure about an event depends on your own point of view as well as the event itself. Observations are *relative* to the frame of reference, or viewpoint, of the observer.

Relativity also applies to larger events in the universe. For example, we can tell how fast our planet is moving only if we

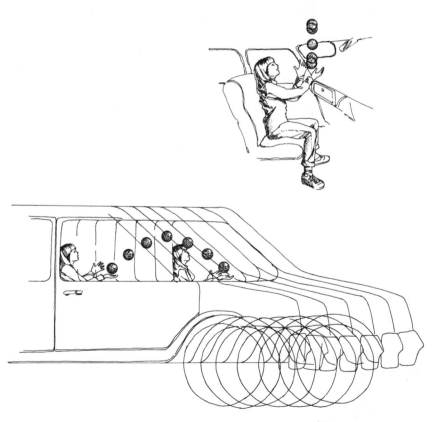

The ball appears to move differently, depending on whether you are viewing it from inside or outside the car.

compare it to something else. Imagine a single planet in a completely empty universe. How fast is it moving? In what direction is it going? Unless we can compare it to some other object, those questions are meaningless.

Around 1900 a young German physicist named Albert Einstein wondered about relativity. How does it affect objects traveling at very high speeds? Light travels *very* fast: 300,000 kilometers per second in a vacuum. Einstein wondered what light waves would look like to a person traveling at the speed of light. He realized that one possible answer might be that the light would seem to be standing still (just as the person sitting next to you in the moving car seems to be sitting still).

But Einstein also realized that that answer didn't make sense. Light is made of waves, and waves must *move* to exist. So he decided to explore another possibility. He saw that the speed of light must *always* be 300,000 kilometers per second, no matter how fast someone is moving when he or she observes it.

Einstein's law that the speed of light is always constant doesn't seem odd at first. But it doesn't fit our everyday, commonsense view of nature. The velocities of everything else in our world work by addition and subtraction. For example, suppose you are riding in a car at 50 miles per hour. You throw an apple core out the window at 10 miles per hour. The total velocity of the apple core must be 60 miles per hour.

Athletes use this principle whenever they throw a ball. When a center fielder has to make a quick throw to home plate, he runs a couple of steps before he winds up and releases his throw. That way the ball has the velocity from his throwing arm *plus* the extra velocity of his running speed as he lets the ball go.

Now imagine two stars, one moving toward Earth at 100,000 kilometers per second and one moving away at the same rate. Both stars are producing light, with the speed of 300,000 kilometers per second. If light acted like other things in our everyday world, we would expect the light from the first star to be moving toward us at 400,000 kilometers per second and the light from

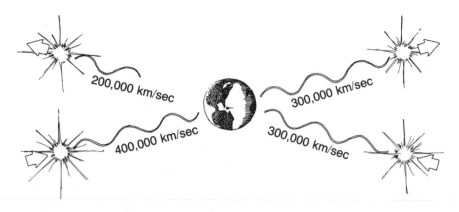

The speed of light is always the same, no matter how fast the source of the light may be moving either toward or away from us.

the other to be moving toward us at 200,000 kilometers per second. That would seem perfectly sensible.

The trouble is, that isn't what happens. Scientists in the 1800s and early 1900s tried and tried to measure differences in the speed of light resulting from the motion of the Earth and stars. The most famous of these experiments was conducted by Albert Michelson and Edward Morley. No matter how carefully scientists designed and carried out their experiments, light always measured 300,000 kilometers per second. It was one of the great scientific puzzles of the time.

Most physicists thought the experiments must not have been designed correctly or that the instruments used to make the measurements weren't accurate enough. But Einstein realized that the experiments had been right all along. The experimenters couldn't measure any differences in the speed of light because light always travels at the same rate. Einstein understood that this must be a basic rule of the universe.

The universal "speed limit" of light seems fairly simple. But Einstein saw that if light always travels at a constant speed, the many other rules of the universe that we considered "common sense" would have to change. Relativity predicted results that seem strange and very different from our everyday experiences. The mathematical calculations that explained these odd realities to Einstein were very difficult. But every one of Einstein's predictions have been proved true since his work was first published in 1905.

One of the most interesting ideas to come from Einstein's law is called time dilation. Time, as viewed by an outside observer, "slows down" as an object moves faster. Imagine a spaceship zooming past the Earth at 200,000 kilometers per second. If we on Earth could somehow see the clocks on that ship, they would seem to be moving much too slowly. Imagine that the people on the spaceship could see Earth at the same time. They would see our planet flashing by at 200,000 kilometers per second. Everything on their ship would seem perfectly normal to them. And from their point of view, our clocks on Earth would seem much too slow!

This strange stretching out, or *dilation,* of time has been proved to happen in experiments. Tiny subatomic particles called muons exist for only two-millionths of a second before they disintegrate. But when they are moving near the speed of light, they last much longer. Their time is stretched out because of their speed.

Another very important part of Einstein's discovery was that energy and mass (matter) are interchangeable. Matter can be changed into energy, and energy can become matter. (We'll learn more about this in Chapter 21.) Relativity tells us that when an object is accelerated closer and closer to the speed of light, it gains more and more mass. This has also been seen in experiments. Physicists give atomic particles, like protons or electrons, huge boosts of speed in giant particle accelerators, or *atom smashers.* As these particles get nearer the speed of light, they actually do gain more mass.

This gain in mass means that space travel at the speed of light is not possible. Newton's Second Law of Motion says that the more mass an object has, the more force is needed to accelerate it. If an object like a spaceship gains more mass as it gets closer to light speed, then it will require more and more force to accelerate further. An object at light speed would have an infinite (limitless) amount of mass. That means it would require an infinite amount of force to continue to accelerate it. Of course, no engine can develop infinite force. So space travelers will always have to be satisfied with slower-than-light travel.

Mass can also be changed into energy. That is exactly what happens in a nuclear reactor or a nuclear bomb. A small amount of uranium or plutonium metal is converted into energy, mostly heat and light. If this event is controlled, the heat can be used to generate electricity. If it happens all at once, it creates a huge explosion.

The part of Einstein's law that tells us that the speed of light is constant for any observer is known as *special relativity*. That's because it deals with the special case of constant, unaccelerated motion. In 1916 Einstein published another portion of his laws of relativity, known as *general relativity*. This part of Einstein's laws gives a new and better explanation for the force of gravity.

General relativity tells us that there is no difference between gravity and acceleration. At least, there is no difference that we can see, feel, or measure.

Imagine yourself in an enclosed spaceship with no windows or other way of finding out what is going on in the space outside it. Your spaceship is accelerating with a constant force of 1 G (the same amount of force as Earth's gravity). When you stand on the floor of your ship, you feel your weight press down on your feet just as it would if you were on Earth. The force of the acceleration pushes you against the floor, just as you are pushed back into your seat when a car accelerates. If you step on a scale, it will read the same weight as on Earth, because the force of acceleration will be pushing the floor of the ship against your body's mass. If you drop a ball, it will "fall" to the floor as the floor of the ship accelerates to meet it. In every way it will seem that a "force" is pulling everything "down" in the direction opposite from the acceleration.

A person in an enclosed, smoothly accelerating spaceship would experience a "downward" pressure that would feel just like the Earth's gravity.

In fact, in a completely closed ship there is no way of telling whether you are accelerating through space at 1 G or just standing on a launch pad on Earth. The effects of gravity are exactly like the effects of uniform (perfectly smooth, constant) acceleration. Einstein's Law of General Relativity tells us that from a particular point of view, there is no difference between gravitation and acceleration.

Einstein's law tells us that we must think of time and space in a new way. We usually think of space as a uniform three-dimensional grid. That means that the location of every object is specified with three dimensions: length, width, and height. Relativity tells us that we must also consider a fourth dimension: time. Every object is constantly moving through a *space-time continuum*. To locate any object, we must say *when* it is as a part of *where* it is. Like the other dimensions, measurements of time depend on your point of view. People moving at different rates will have different measurements of time!

Einstein also tells us that the objects themselves affect the shape of the space-time continuum in which they are located. We can't think of space as just an empty graph-paper-like grid anymore. The shape of space and time depends on the objects in it. Very large objects such as stars have noticeable effects on the shape of space and time. A huge star actually "bends" or "warps" the shape of the space-time around it. "Straight" lines in space curve toward large masses such as planets or stars.

Try to picture space-time as a stretchy fishnet. Wherever there is a large object, the fishnet sags. Smaller objects nearby naturally roll toward the large objects. The distortions that masses cause in the shape of space-time result in what we call gravity. The "force" of gravity doesn't come from masses, but from the shape of space itself.

Einstein predicted that gravitation should even bend light if his laws were correct. A mass large enough to bend light is called a *gravitational lens*. It actually happens. The sun, for example, is massive enough to bend space-time and act as a gravita-

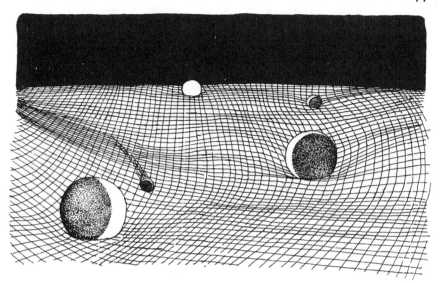

Einstein realized that large masses affect the shape of space and time.

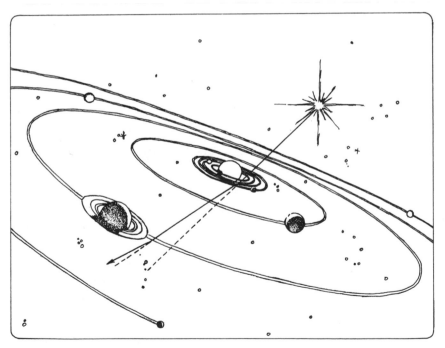

The gravitational force of the sun is strong enough to bend the light from a distant star.

tional lens. The effect has been observed during eclipses. Stars seen near the sun during eclipses appear to be out of position, because their light has been bent by the sun's gravity.

Relativity also predicted the existence of *black holes*. A black hole is a tremendously massive object, like a burned-out star. A black hole is so massive that it bends light back into itself. The light can never escape. Since no light ever leaves a black hole, we can never see one. But astronomers have detected huge concentrations of energy in space, which are evidence of these strange objects.

Another strange result of relativity is that gravitation affects time. The closer you are to a large mass, the more slowly time moves. Experiments here on Earth have shown that this actually happens. Extremely accurate atomic clocks move more slowly at sea level than they do at the top of a high building. The difference in time is due to the weakening of gravity as the clock is moved farther from the center of the Earth. Time slows down even more near huge objects like stars. And scientists believe that at the surface of a black hole, time stops completely!

In our century Einstein's laws have "replaced" Newton's laws of motion and gravitation. They are the best description of how gravitation and motion work in our universe. That doesn't mean that Newton was wrong. Newton's laws still work perfectly for objects moving at comparatively low speeds. But Einstein showed us that objects and energies behave differently when they travel at or near the speed of light.

Like Newton, Einstein made many important contributions to physics. Like Newton, he made many of his important discoveries when he was very young. Einstein was only twenty-six years old when his first description of relativity was published. And, like Newton, Albert Einstein received many honors for his contributions to human knowledge. In 1921 he won the Nobel Prize for physics. Much of his later life was spent working for world peace. By the time of his death in 1955, he was loved and respected throughout the world.

20.
QUANTUM MECHANICS

Mechanics is the study of motion. It is the branch of physics that tells us how the familiar objects of our world move and interact with one another. The laws of *classical mechanics* include Newton's three laws of motion and Galileo's Law of Uniform Acceleration. These laws all seem sensible to us. That's because they tell us about the motions of ordinary objects of familiar size. Whenever we see the objects in our world move, they follow the laws of classical mechanics.

Atoms and atomic particles, however, follow a different set of rules as they move and therefore need a different set of laws. The branch of physics that studies the motion of atoms is known as *quantum mechanics*. Scientists have discovered that the laws of quantum mechanics are very different from the laws of classical mechanics, which describe our everyday world.

Before 1897, when J. J. Thomson discovered the electron, scientists thought that atoms were the smallest possible pieces of matter. But Thomson's discovery proved that this wasn't true. Atoms themselves were made of smaller, subatomic particles. Ernest Rutherford discovered the proton in the early 1900s, and the neutron was discovered by James Chadwick in 1932.

Protons, neutrons, and electrons are the three main particles that make up all atoms. But dozens of other atomic particles have also been found to exist. Atoms turn out to have a complicated structure of their own. New subatomic particles are still being discovered today.

When John Dalton first discovered that matter is made of atoms, most scientists expected atoms to follow the same rules of motion as larger pieces of matter. But an electron or a proton is nothing like a baseball or a boulder or a planet. Atomic particles don't follow the same laws that larger objects do. New laws of physics were needed to describe the behavior of electrons and other atomic particles. The laws of quantum mechanics were written because physicists needed to describe the actions of those particles. The early 1900s were one of the most exciting times in the history of science because so many brilliant scientists were working together to solve the mysteries of how atoms work.

Quantum mechanics is one of the most important areas of modern physics. It is so different from our everyday experiences, however, that we can't do experiments with ordinary objects to show how quantum laws work. Quantum laws apply only to matter the size of atoms and smaller. To help you understand how quantum mechanics is different from the classical mechanics of our everyday world, try to picture the following imaginary example:

Imagine an ordinary garden hose attached to an ordinary water faucet. When you turn on the faucet just a little, a trickle of water begins to flow through the hose. A small amount of water dribbles out of the nozzle. As you gradually turn the faucet handle, more and more water flows through the hose. The nozzle gradually sprays water farther and farther. By adjusting the amount of water flowing from the faucet, you can make the water spray ½ meter, 4 meters, 7.8 meters, or whatever other distance you choose. That is how a sprinkler works according to classical mechanics.

Now imagine another hose. This time, as you slowly and gradually turn on the faucet, nothing happens. No water comes out of the nozzle, not even a dribble. Then, when you turn the faucet to a certain point, the hose starts spraying water. But it sprays in a very special way. The water sprays out in

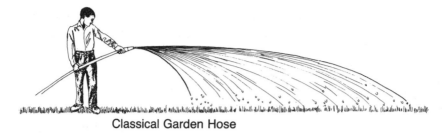

Classical Garden Hose

Quantum Garden Hose

A "classical" garden hose sprays water in the ordinary way. But an imaginary "quantum" hose would only spray water drops with certain specific amounts of force.

droplets of *exactly* 1 milliliter each, which land *exactly* 1 meter away.

You turn the faucet handle farther, but the hose continues to spray only at the 1-meter distance. Then, all of a sudden, the spray jumps out to a distance of 2 meters. None of the water lands between the 1-meter and 2-meter marks. One moment the spray reaches 1 meter, and the next it reaches 2 meters.

As you gradually increase the flow of water from the faucet, the same "jumps" keep happening. The water will spray only at whole-number distances. And it always sprays droplets of exactly 1 milliliter each. The spray is not continuous. Instead, the nozzle sprays only in certain allowable distances and amounts. Those amounts could be called *quanta*, and this odd hose would be a *quantum* garden hose.

Obviously, this sort of strange behavior doesn't really happen with garden hoses. But it does happen with electrons. It's called the *photoelectric effect,* and it was a great mystery to the physicists of 1900.

When light shines on certain metals, it causes an electric current. That is known as the photoelectric effect. (*Photo-* is the Greek prefix meaning *light.*) You may have already experienced this effect without realizing it. It's what makes an electric-eye door open and close. In an electric eye, a thin beam of light shines on a special metal plate. As long as the light is shining onto the metal receiver, electricity flows. But when someone walks by, the light is interrupted, just as it is when you put your hand between a movie projector and the screen. Interrupting the beam of light stops the flow of electricity, triggering a motor that opens the door.

The photoelectric effect is also used to generate electricity from sunlight. Special solar cells generate an electric current when light shines down on them. You may have seen photoelectric cells like this on "solar-powered" calculators.

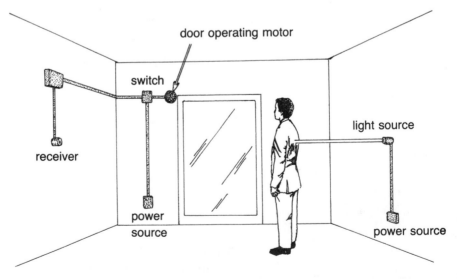

When the man interrupts the beam of light hitting a photoelectric cell, a switch turns on the motor, opening the door.

You might expect that the brighter the light shining on the metal, the more energy the electrons will have. But it doesn't work that way. As you increase the amount of light shining on a photoelectric cell, the amount of electrical current produced will increase. But the voltage (or energy level) will not change. It's as if we turned up the water flow in our garden hose and more water came out the nozzle, but it didn't spray any farther than it did when there were just a few drops flowing through the hose.

Physicists experimenting with photoelectric metal found that some light won't produce any electric current at all. For example, red light won't cause any electrons to flow, no matter how

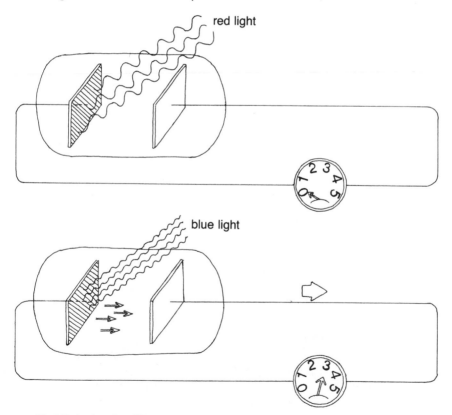

Red light (top) *will not cause a current to flow in a photoelectric cell, but blue light* (bottom) *will.*

bright it is. However, even a very dim blue light will generate some electrical current. But the most surprising result was that when the brightness of the blue light is increased, the energy level of the flowing electrons stays the same.

Scientists expected the photoelectric effect to work like the "classical" garden hose described earlier. The more light they shone on the metal, the more voltage they expected to get. But that's not what happened. Instead, the photoelectric effect works like our imaginary "quantum" garden hose. Either you get electrons with certain specific amounts of electrical energy or none at all.

Why does electricity flow in a piece of metal just because light is shining on it? Electricity is the movement of tiny particles called electrons. How can light cause those particles to move? And why does dim blue light make electrons flow, when much brighter red light does not? And most of all, why do the electrons have only certain energy levels as they flow through the metal? That was the mystery of the photoelectric effect.

Two German scientists, Max Planck and Albert Einstein, finally solved the mystery. And with their work, quantum mechanics was born. Einstein and Planck proved that atoms and their particles—electrons, protons, and neutrons—follow different rules from the large chunks of matter that we are familiar with in our daily lives. In just a few years of rapid scientific advancement, there was a new set of laws about how the smallest bits of matter behave.

In 1900 Planck was studying the problem of how light radiates from a glowing object. He discovered that light waves can have only certain whole-number amounts of energy. The energy of any light wave *had* to be a multiple of a certain extremely small number. That number, usually represented by the letter *h*, is known as *Planck's constant*. It is a very important number. Planck's constant is the basic size limit for any energy in the universe, just as the speed of light is the basic speed limit.

Planck's law says that the energy of light is directly proportional to its frequency. Mathematically, it is written like this:

$$\text{Energy} = h \times \text{frequency} \quad or \quad E = h \times f$$

In Planck's equation E is the energy of a certain wavelength of light. Planck's constant is h, and f is the frequency of the light. Frequency tells how rapidly the light wave vibrates (vibrations per second). Light waves with higher frequencies vibrate more often in a given amount of time. Higher frequency light also has shorter wavelengths than lower frequency light. That's because high frequency light vibrates more often in the same amount of distance.

Planck's equation tells us that the higher the frequency (and the smaller the wavelength) of light, the more energy it has. For example, blue light has a higher frequency than red light. So blue light waves have higher energies than red light waves.

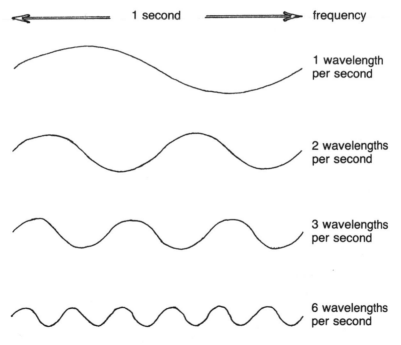

Light waves with higher frequencies also have shorter wavelengths. If the waves are shorter, more wave crests will pass by a certain point in the same amount of time.

But Planck's discovery says something else too. Light may act like a wave, but it comes only in specific amounts of energy. Light always comes in little "chunks" or "bits." Because light energy only comes in exact amounts, it has to be considered a particle! Planck called each little chunk of light a *quantum* (plural: *quanta*).

A few years after Planck's discovery, Albert Einstein was working on the problem of the photoelectric effect. He realized that he could use Planck's discovery to explain what happens: Electrons can absorb only light waves with certain amounts of energy. A light wave either gives an electron enough energy to "jump free" from its atom or none at all. The light acts like particles, not waves. Either an electron absorbs a whole quantum of light or none. An electron cannot absorb part of the energy of a light particle. If the light has enough energy, it knocks the electron away from its atom and starts an electric current. If the light doesn't have enough energy, nothing happens at all.

Einstein called the light particles *photons*. The photons of red light simply don't have enough energy to bump the electrons away from their atoms. So no matter how much red light shines on the metal, no current will be generated. Photons of blue light have a shorter wavelength. (Remember that higher frequency equals shorter wavelength.) So blue photons have more energy. They are powerful enough to generate a current. That is true even in very dim light. Dim blue light has fewer photons, but each photon still has all the energy of blue light.

Max Planck received the Nobel Prize in 1918 for his discovery that light comes in whole-number amounts of energy, or quanta. Three years later Albert Einstein won the Nobel Prize for his explanation of the photoelectric effect.

The discoveries of Planck and Einstein provided an answer to one of the longest scientific disputes in history: Is light a particle or a wave? In the 1600s Isaac Newton's study of light convinced him that it is made up of many tiny particles. But Christiaan Huygens argued that light behaves like a wave. Since that time scientists studying light have collected evidence to support each idea. Most experiments showed that light behaves like a wave. But there were others that showed that light acts more like a stream of particles. Which was correct? Is light a wave or is it a particle?

Quantum mechanics has finally given us the answer. Is light a wave or a particle? The answer is: both! Light must be considered as both a wave and a particle. It usually behaves like a wave, but it comes in specific-sized bits, like particles.

Since the early 1900s many more advances have been made in quantum mechanics. This modern physics explains many events that happen because of the behavior of atoms and atomic particles.

One thing that quantum mechanics explains is how atoms combine to form chemical compounds. In 1913 the Danish physicist Niels Bohr created a picture of the atom that explained the properties of different elements. You are probably familiar with his idea of atomic structure. Bohr saw the atom as a tiny central nucleus surrounded by orbiting electrons. The nucleus

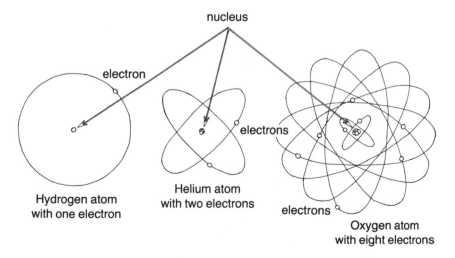

Bohr suggested that electrons orbit the nucleus of an atom in "shells." The oxygen atom (right) *has an inner and an outer electron shell.*

is made of protons and neutrons and has a positive charge. The negatively charged electrons orbit around the nucleus in "shells" having different energy levels.

According to Bohr's theory, the electrons in the outer shell of an atom can be shared with other atoms. In this way, atoms bond together to form molecules. Only the outer electrons of any atom are free to combine with other atoms in chemical reactions.

Bohr also said that an atom can have no more than eight electrons in its outermost shell. This explained why the elements follow the pattern of properties described by Mendeleev's periodic table. Mendeleev's arrangement of atoms has eight basic families. The elements in each family all have the same number of electrons in their outer shells. For his contributions to the understanding of atomic structure, Bohr received the Nobel Prize in 1922.

But Bohr's idea was just the beginning. Physicists continued to improve their description of how the atom works. Although electrons and other parts of atoms are usually thought of as particles, they often behave like waves. In the mid-1920s Louis Vidor, Prince de Broglie and Erwin Schrödinger showed that electrons vibrate around the atom in a pattern of waves. What Bohr called orbits were actually wave patterns. Only certain wave patterns "fit" around the nucleus of each atom.

Other atomic particles act like waves as well. In the world of the atom, it's impossible to distinguish between waves and particles. Light can be a particle, and electrons are matter-waves!

Each kind of atom has a certain number of precise wave patterns its electrons can follow. An electron "jumps" to a higher energy wave pattern when it absorbs a photon of energy. It emits, or sends out, a photon of light when it jumps back to a lower energy level. The energy that an electron emits as light must equal the amount of energy it absorbs from photons. So the total amount of energy stays the same. The Law of Conservation of Energy applies even to the energy of a single atom!

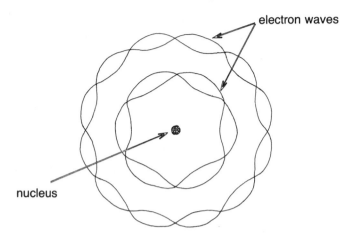

Modern physicists picture electrons as patterns of waves vibrating around the atomic nucleus.

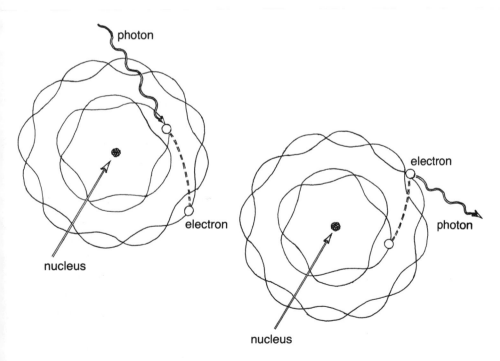

When atoms absorb or emit photons of light, their electrons "jump" from one energy level to another.

Here are two other examples of how quantum laws have helped scientists understand our universe.

As an element gets hot, it radiates energy in the form of light. For example, the gases in a candle flame are hot enough to give off yellow light. The gases in our sun also glow brightly, giving off tremendous amounts of light energy.

Each chemical element radiates light only at certain wavelengths. That's because the atoms of each element have their own special arrangement of electron wave patterns. Each element has its own unmistakable set of wavelengths that it produces as it glows. Because of this, the light that elements give off when heated can be used to identify them.

The instrument that scientists use to examine the spectrum of light is called a *spectroscope*. If you shine the light from a glowing gas through a spectroscope, it breaks up into all the different wavelengths of light being emitted by the gas. Since each element has its own special set of wavelengths, a spectroscope can be used to identify all the elements in a sample of glowing gas.

Spectroscopes are so sensitive that they can even recognize the elements in the light of a distant star. In fact, the element helium wasn't discovered here on Earth. It was first found with a spectroscope in the spectrum of the sun. By examining the spectra of stars, scientists can see that the very same elements found on Earth are also found throughout the universe. This means that the same physical and chemical laws that apply here on Earth must apply everywhere else in the universe as well.

Quantum laws also explain what happens inside the fluorescent light bulbs in your home. Fluorescent lights are filled with a gas. When house current flows through the gas, it boosts the energy of some of the electrons in the gas atoms. The electrons emit photons as they vibrate with the added energy. Those photons hit a special coating on the inside surface of the lightbulb. Electrons in this coating absorb these photons and then re-emit them as the visible light we see.

Before we leave this chapter, let's summarize the rules of quantum mechanics:

- The laws of motion that apply to large objects do not apply to atomic particles.
- The smaller the wavelength of light, the more energy it has.
- Energy (including light) always comes in specific-sized bits, which we call quanta or photons.
- Light acts like a particle as well as a wave.
- Electrons and other subatomic particles act like waves as well as particles.

21.

CONSERVATION OF MASS/ENERGY

Whenever changes take place in our universe, certain things must remain constant. The laws that tell us *what* remains constant are known as the laws of conservation.

In the late 1700s Antoine Lavoisier proved that when substances change form in chemical reactions, the total amount of matter (or mass) must still remain the same. That law is known as the Law of Conservation of Matter (Chapter 9). In the mid 1800s James Joule proved that energy could be converted from one form to another, but the total amount of energy in any reaction always remains the same. That law is known as the Law of Conservation of Energy (Chapter 15). Both of these laws were very important in the history of science.

However, in the early 1900s Albert Einstein gave scientists a new understanding of matter and energy. This new viewpoint was found in Einstein's most famous equation:

$$E = mc^2$$

Chances are you have heard of this equation or seen it. But you may not know what it means. Einstein's equation is read: "*E* equals *mc* squared." *E*, in this equation, stands for energy, *m* stands for mass, and *c* is the speed of light.

This little equation is a mathematical way of stating a very *big* idea. It says that matter and energy are actually different forms of the same thing! Matter can be converted into energy and energy can be converted into matter. In a way, you could think of all the matter in our universe as "frozen energy."

Pick up a pencil or a match, or look at your little finger. Whatever piece of matter that you look at is composed of billions of tiny atoms. Each atom is vibrating with energy. Energy holds the atoms in place. Energy connects the atoms with one another to form molecules. And energy even holds the tiny subatomic particles together to form the atoms themselves. Each atom is a whirling, pulsing clump of energy we call matter.

Einstein's equation tells us that there is a *tremendous* amount of energy locked up in even the tiniest bits of matter. The equation tells us how to figure out how much energy (E) there is in a piece of matter. We must multiply the amount of matter (m) by the speed of light (c) squared. Remember that squaring a number means multiplying it by itself.

The speed of light is a very large number. Squaring the speed of light means multiplying the speed of light times the speed of light. That gives us an enormous number. If we could somehow release *all* the energy in a single gram of matter, we would have a tremendous amount of energy. One gram of matter is equal to more than 21 billion calories of energy! That is as much energy as the energy released by burning 3,000 tons of coal.

Einstein's equation also tells us that if we gave an object more energy, we could increase its mass. But to do this, we would have to add tremendous amounts of extra energy.

You may be wondering if these events are actually possible. Could we really change a piece of matter into energy? Could we somehow turn energy into matter? The answer is yes. Both things have been done here on Earth during the last forty years.

Scientists have changed energy into mass in giant *particle accelerators* that are used in modern physics research. A particle accelerator is a huge machine that boosts the speed of tiny atomic particles almost to the speed of light. These accelerators are circular tubes, sometimes miles long. Atomic particles are held in these tubes and speeded up with electromagnetic force. The atomic particles, such as protons or electrons, whirl around the ring of tubes at enormous speeds. The tubes have no air in them, and so the particles have no atoms to collide against. Each time they zoom around the ring they are given another boost of power with an electromagnetic field. They go a little

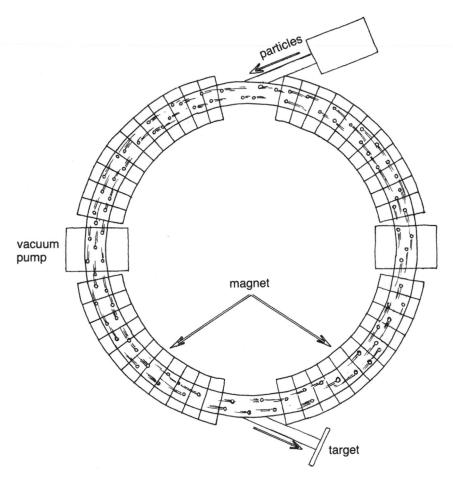

In an accelerator, atomic particles speed through an empty tube, controlled by many magnets. When they are moving fast enough, the particles are directed toward a target.

faster with each boost. Powerful magnets keep the particles from flying out through the walls of the tube.

After they've traveled around the tube millions of times and received millions of energy boosts, the particles are traveling at almost the speed of light. Because of their speed, they have tremendous energy. The beam of particles is then aimed at a target.

Of course, the atomic particles are much too fast and much too small to see. So physicists use the evidence they leave behind when they hit the target to find out about them. Researchers keep a careful photographic record of what happens to the target as the particles hit.

Imagine that you arrive at the scene of an accident. A vehicle has crashed into a wall, but the vehicle has been towed away. You know the vehicle that hit the wall was moving at 30 miles per hour. It should be easy for you to tell whether the vehicle was a bicycle, a small car, or a 10-ton truck. Just look at how much damage has been done. A truck will certainly cause much more destruction than a bicycle.

Scientists study the results of the collisions in their accelerators in a similar way. They can't see the speeding particles, but they know how much energy the particles have been given as they were accelerated. The scientists can study the evidence that the collisions of the particles leave behind. For example, from studying the photographs of very fast protons hitting their targets, scientists can tell that these particles have more mass than ordinary protons. The energy that they received as they accelerated to tremendous speeds has been converted into extra mass! So particle accelerators have actually managed to turn tremendous amounts of energy into tiny bits of matter.

What about turning matter into energy? That has been done too, in nuclear reactors and nuclear bombs.

A nuclear bomb uses about 10 kilograms of uranium or pluto-nium metal for fuel. In a nuclear reaction the atoms of fuel split apart, forming atoms of other elements. When an atom splits, some of its mass is released as energy. When a nuclear bomb explodes, about 1/1000 of its nuclear fuel is converted from matter into energy. So a "small" atomic bomb explodes with the force of only 10 grams of matter! But the energy in it creates the enormous explosion and blast of the bomb.

The same conversion of matter into energy takes place in a nuclear reactor. In a reactor the conversion from matter to energy is carefully controlled to avoid an explosion. The radioactive fuel in a nuclear reactor is extremely dangerous to handle. But suppose you could weigh the fuel that's put into a reactor, allow it to run for a year, and then weigh the fuel again. You would find that a small fraction of the weight would have disappeared. Some of the uranium in the reactor would have been converted to the heat that is then used to generate electricity. But even in a nuclear reactor or a tremendous nuclear explosion, mass is not completely converted to energy. Only a small portion of the energy "frozen" in the matter is released as energy. The rest remains in the form of atoms and atomic particles.

The sun also changes mass into energy. The sun is a giant nuclear reactor, constantly transforming part of its mass into energy. We receive some of that energy here on Earth as sunlight.

You can even see mass transformed into energy right before your eyes. Just light a match. Tiny quantities of mass are converted to energy even in ordinary chemical reactions. When a match burns, a minute amount of the match's mass is released as energy. We see that energy as light and heat. But the amount of mass that becomes energy is so tiny that not even the most sensitive scale could measure it.

Einstein's equation shows that mass can be changed into energy and energy can be changed into mass. So we can no longer say that the total amount of mass still remains the same in every reaction. Some mass is "lost." It becomes energy! And we can no longer say that the total amount of energy in any reaction always remains the same. Some energy may be converted to mass! The Law of Conservation of Matter and the Law of Conservation of Energy are not quite true.

Matter and energy are equivalent. Matter is simply energy in a different form. So we must combine the two laws into one. Scientists now use the Law of Conservation of Mass/Energy. It says that the total amount of mass and energy in any reaction must remain the same. Mass may be converted to energy or energy may be converted to mass, but no mass or energy can be created or destroyed.

All those changes came from Einstein's simple little equation:

$$E = mc^2$$

It has given us a whole new way of looking at our universe and ourselves.

22.
THE UNCERTAINTY PRINCIPLE

The instruments of science have become better and better over the past four hundred years. Scientific measurements have become more and more accurate. In the early 1900s it seemed as if anything scientists wanted to know could be measured. It was just a matter of making a measuring device that was accurate enough and then using it to "look" at whatever was to be measured. In the early 1900s what scientists most wanted to look at were atomic particles.

In studying a moving object, you need two pieces of information. You need to know the object's current location and its momentum. Remember that momentum is a measurement of the *amount* of motion of an object. It includes both the object's mass and its velocity. If you know an object's location and momentum, you can then predict what it will do as it *continues* its motion. Picture a bowling ball rolling down an alley. Suppose that, at a particular moment, you know exactly where it is. You also know exactly how fast it's moving and in what direction. If you know these two things, you can predict exactly where the ball will hit when it reaches the end of the alley.

In the early 1900s scientists wanted to find out exactly what was happening inside an atom. How fast did the electrons move, and exactly where were they located in an atom? Just as for measuring any other moving object, physicists needed two pieces of information about an electron. They needed to know its position and its momentum.

Now think about what actually happens when we look at something. First of all, we need a source of light. This might be a lamp or a flashlight or the sun. Light waves from our light source hit the object we are observing and bounce back to our eye. Our eye senses the light that hits it and sends an image to our brain.

The same thing happens when we take a picture with a camera. We still need a light source, an object to observe, and a piece of film to record the image. As a rule, to make any observation we must have three things: an object to observe, some light to bounce off the object, and an observing instrument, like an eye or a camera.

If you look at something large, like a chair or a tree or a dog, shining a little light on it doesn't affect it very much. But something strange happens when you try to "look" at an electron. Suppose we try to look at an electron with ordinary light.

Visible light has a wavelength about ten thousand times larger than the width of an *atom*. And a single electron is much, much smaller than a whole atom. When we try to "see" an electron by hitting it with ordinary light, we find that it is impossible. The light waves are so much larger than the electron that we can't get any picture at all. They simply miss the target. We can get no idea of where the electron is or how fast it is moving.

But perhaps we can see an electron if we use a different kind of light. To get a clearer picture of the electron, we need to use light with a much smaller wavelength. That way, the light waves won't "miss" the electron so badly. Instead, they will bounce off the electrons and come back to be recorded on a camera. X-rays and gamma rays have much smaller wavelengths than visible light. They can also be used to take a photograph. Why not shine X-rays on an electron and take a picture of its location that way?

The problem with this is that X-rays and gamma rays have very high energy. Planck showed that the energy of light increases as its wavelength decreases. X-rays are so very powerful

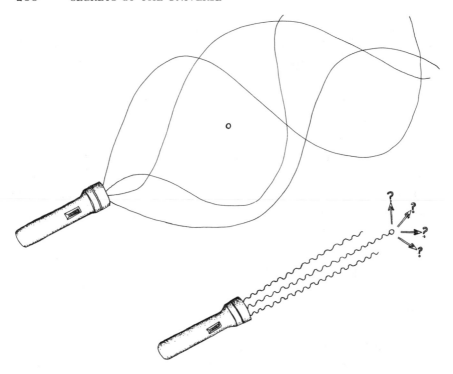

Low-energy light waves are too large to locate an atomic particle like an electron. High-energy light waves hit the particle hard enough to knock it away in unpredictable directions.

that when one of these light waves hits an electron, it knocks it completely off course. It totally changes the electron's speed and direction. The X-ray may bounce back to a camera and tell us where the electron *was* at the moment when it was hit. But there is no way to predict where it is now and where it's going.

Looking at an electron with X-rays is a little like trying to find out where a golf ball is by throwing tennis balls at it. Imagine that you are in a completely dark room. You know that somewhere in front of you is a golf ball. You have a supply of tennis balls. You toss the tennis balls out into the dark, keeping careful track of exactly where you throw each one. Eventually one of your tennis balls hits the golf ball squarely and bounces right back to you. Now you know where the golf ball *was* when you made your throw. But where is it now? You have no idea. In locating the golf ball, the tennis ball has knocked it away somewhere. You can only guess where it might have gone.

When we look for electrons with very high-energy light waves, we can get a sharper picture of an electron's location. But just by observing the electron, we have caused a change in its momentum. In fact, atomic particles cannot be observed without disturbing them. That means there must always be some uncertainty about where atomic particles are and what they are doing. We will never be able to know *everything* about an electron or a proton or a neutron. They will always look fuzzy to us. This rule is known as the Uncertainty Principle.

This law was discovered by Werner Heisenberg in 1927. It is known as the Heisenberg Uncertainty Principle. The Uncertainty Principle can be stated like this: It is impossible to measure atomic particles without disturbing the particles. Therefore it is never possible to know everything there is to know about these particles.

Perhaps this is not surprising, since atomic particles are wave-like in their behavior. De Broglie and Schrödinger showed that

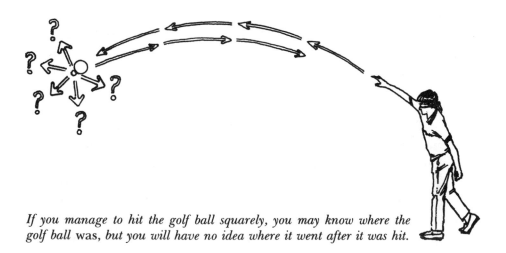

If you manage to hit the golf ball squarely, you may know where the golf ball was, *but you will have no idea where it went after it was hit.*

electrons can best be thought of as matter-waves vibrating around the nucleus of an atom. We wouldn't expect a wave to have a single fixed position. Atoms are often pictured as miniature solar systems, with electron "planets" orbiting a nucleus "sun." But the Uncertainty Principle reminds us that this is only a picture to help us get an idea of something that is impossible to see. An atom is *not* a miniature solar system. And its actions follow a different set of rules. The most accurate picture of an atom that we can imagine is a fuzzy set of probable locations and velocities for the atom's particles. These locations and speeds are only *likely*, not certain.

The Heisenberg Uncertainty Principle is a very important idea. It tells us that no matter how accurate or careful our scientific measurements become, we can never know everything about the universe. If nothing else, there will always be uncertainty about the actions of atomic particles. We can never be sure what they are doing at any given time. The best that physicists can do is to determine where an electron is *most likely* to be at any time, and how fast it is *most likely* to be moving.

Heisenberg's Uncertainty Principle is a law that applies to the actions of atomic particles. But the idea is an important one for other sciences too. All scientists need to remember that observing something often has an effect on the thing that they are observing. Therefore it may be impossible to observe any event in perfectly natural, undisturbed conditions.

For example, biologists often look through a microscope at tiny creatures in a drop of water. But the very act of looking at those creatures can change their behavior. They have been removed from their environment and placed in a single drop of water on a glass slide. A microscope focuses extra light on the subjects being observed so that they can be seen clearly. The light also raises the temperature of the water. All these changes may affect the actions of the creatures the biologist is observing.

Suppose we wanted to study the activities of forest animals, without the interference of human beings. We could set up an automatic camera in the woods and then leave. Even so, the strange appearance of the camera and its whirring sound might affect the animals' behavior in unexpected ways. Perhaps the scent of the camera or the humans who set it up might also affect what the animals do. No matter how careful we were, we could never be certain that the animals we photographed were behaving in a completely natural way.

Here's one more example from everyday life. Suppose your mother wanted to see how your little brother behaves in kindergarten class. So she decides to visit his class for an hour and watch him work and play. Would you expect your brother's behavior to be exactly the same as it would be if your mother weren't there?

Of course not. Even if your mother just sits quietly and watches, your brother will know that she is watching him. Because she's watching, he might be especially careful about behaving well. Or he might decide to show off to get her attention. Just the fact that your mother is present will affect what she sees.

Heisenberg's Uncertainty Principle tells us that it is impossible for science to understand the universe completely. No matter how carefully we experiment, no matter how accurate our scientific instruments are, some things in the universe will always be hidden from us. Scientists will continue to experiment, in an effort to find the laws that tell us how our universe works. But in a sense, Heisenberg's Uncertainty Principle may be the *last* law of the universe. No matter how wonderful the human brain may be, we can't know everything.

That doesn't mean that we now know all there is to know about the universe. Scientists still have much to learn about the stars and planets, the atom, and the miracles of life. There are still more laws to discover and more mysteries to solve. Perhaps you may one day add your name to that distinguished list of scientists who have helped discover the secrets of the universe.

APPENDIX _____
THE INVERSE SQUARE LAWS

A number of important natural laws all follow a similar pattern. This pattern is known as the *inverse square law*. Gravitational force behaves in this way. So do electrical and magnetic force. So does the intensity of light. It isn't an accident that all these laws are so similar. Here is an explanation of why the inverse square law applies to so many different kinds of forces.

In all inverse square laws, the strength of the force that the law describes is inversely proportional to the distance from the source of the force. When two quantities are inversely proportional, one measurement decreases as the other one increases. In these laws the intensity of the force decreases as the distance increases. In all inverse square laws, however, the intensity decreases in proportion to the *square* of the distance from the center of force.

When you square a number, you multiply it by itself. For example, 5 squared is 5 times 5, or 25; 10 squared is 10 times 10, or 100. The symbol used to indicate that a number is squared is a little 2 placed at the upper right of the number. That 2 is called an *exponent*. It tells you how many times to multiply the bigger number times itself. It looks like this:

$$5^2 = 25$$

The intensity of light follows an inverse square law. The

intensity of light is inversely proportional to the square of the distance from the light source. As you get farther from a light source, the brightness of the light from that source decreases rapidly. Let's use light as an example to see why so many different forces follow this one pattern.

Imagine a source of light, like a tiny electric bulb in the middle of a large, dark space. The light spreads out from the source in all directions, like an expanding bubble.

Light intensity is measured in lumens. Let's suppose our light source is producing a total of 1,000 lumens of light.

Now picture a sphere with a 1-meter radius surrounding the light source. The light from the source now illuminates the inside of the sphere.

How much area does the light have to illuminate? The surface area of a sphere is calculated by multiplying 4 times pi (3.14) times the square of the radius of the sphere.

$$A = 4 \times pi \times r^2$$

So our sphere has a surface area of 12.56 square meters. The 1,000 lumens of light produced by the bulb will be distributed evenly around those 12.56 square meters of sphere.

Dividing the total amount of light into the number of square meters in the sphere will tell us how much light is shining on each square meter. When we divide 1,000 lumens among 12.56 square meters, we find that each square meter is illuminated with about 80 lumens of light.

Suppose we double the radius of the sphere surrounding our light source. You will see that the 1,000 lumens of light get distributed over a much larger area. The new sphere has a radius of 2 meters. To compute the total surface area, again we multiply $4 \times pi \times r^2$. Our new sphere has an area of 50.24 square meters. Notice that the radius of the new sphere is only twice as big as the radius of the first sphere. But the area of the second sphere is *four* times larger than the area of the first. That is because the area of a sphere is based on the *square* of the radius.

Our light source is still producing the same amount of light, 1,000 lumens. But now that same amount of light is shining on a sphere with 50.24 square meters of area. So each square meter only receives about 20 lumens of light.

Notice that this is only one-fourth of the amount that each square meter received in the first sphere. In short, the distance from the light source to the sphere has doubled, but the intensity of the light is only one-fourth as great. This is the inverse square relationship.

The same thing will hold true if the radius is increased to 3 meters. Once again we multiply $4 \times pi \times r^2$. Our third sphere has a surface area of 113.04 square meters. The radius of this sphere is three times as big as the radius of the original sphere, but the area of the third sphere is *nine* times larger.

Now our 1,000 lumens of light are spread out across 113.04 square meters of area. Each square meter of our third sphere receives only about 9 lumens of light. This is only one-ninth of the amount that each square meter received in the first sphere.

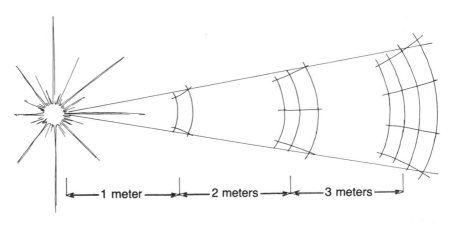

The same amount of light, as it spreads out from a source, fills an increasingly large area.

The distance from the center to the sphere has now tripled, but the intensity of the light is only one-ninth as great.

Total lumens	Radius	Surface area	Lumens per sq m
1,000	1 m	12.56 sq m	80
1,000	2 m	50.24 sq m	20
1,000	3 m	113.04 sq m	9

Of course, the spheres don't actually exist. The imaginary spheres simply give us a way of picturing why the intensity of the light decreases at a much faster rate than the distance increases. It's because the total amount of energy gets spread out over a rapidly expanding area.

You should even be able to see this inverse square law happening with your own eyes. Mark off distances of 10, 20, and 30 meters from a 0 point in your backyard or on the sidewalk near your house. When it gets dark, stand on your 0 point. Ask someone to stand with a flashlight on the 10-meter mark. Look at the intensity of the light. Then have them move to the 20-and 30-meter marks and compare what you see. Although you won't be able to measure the intensity unless you have a very sensitive light meter, you should be able to tell that it is decreasing rapidly as your assistant gets farther away.

You can picture gravitational force spreading out from the center of the Earth (or any other mass) in the same way that light spreads out from a light source. You can picture a magnetic or electrical field spreading outward from a source in a similar way. Picture each force spreading outward from its source like an ever-expanding bubble.

The inverse square relationship holds true for all these forces because they all spread out evenly in all directions from the center point where they are generated. As you get farther and farther away, the effect of these forces is spread over a much larger area.

BIBLIOGRAPHY _____

Books that are of particular interest to young readers are starred.

*Adler, Irving. *The Wonders of Physics: An Introduction to the Physical World.* New York: Golden Press, 1966.

Apfel, Necia H. *It's All Relative: Einstein's Theory of Relativity.* New York: Lothrop, Lee and Shepard, 1981.

Asimov, Isaac. *Asimov's New Guide to Science.* New York: Basic Books, 1984.

———. *The History of Physics.* New York: Walker and Co., 1966.

———. *The Search for the Elements.* New York: Basic Books, 1962.

*Beiser, Germaine, and Arthur Beiser. *Physics for Everybody.* New York: E. P. Dutton, 1956.

*———. *The Story of Gravity.* New York: E. P. Dutton, 1968.

Calder, Nigel. *Einstein's Universe.* New York: Viking Press, 1979.

*Chisholm, Jane, and Mary Johnson. *Usborne Introduction to Chemistry.* Usborne Publishing Ltd., 1983.

Cline, Barbara Lovett. *The Questioners: Physicists and the Quantum Theory.* New York: Thomas Y. Crowell, 1965.

Einstein, Albert. *Relativity, The Special and General Theory.* New York: Crown, 1961.

*Ellis, R. Hobart. *Knowing the Atomic Nucleus.* New York: Lothrop, Lee and Shepard, 1973.

*Fisher, David E. *The Ideas of Einstein.* New York: Holt, Rinehart and Winston, 1980.

*Freeman, Ira M. *Light and Radiation*. New York: Random House, 1965.

*Galant, Roy A. *Explorers of the Atom*. New York: Doubleday, 1974.

Gamow, George. *Biography of Physics*. New York: Harper & Row, 1961.

———. *One, Two, Three . . . Infinity*. New York: Viking Press, 1961.

*Goldstein-Jackson, Kevin. *Experiments with Everyday Objects: Science Activities for Children, Parents and Teachers*. Englewood Cliffs, N. J.: Prentice-Hall, 1978.

Gribbin, John. *In Search of Schrödinger's Cat: Quantum Physics and Reality*. New York: Bantam Books, 1984.

*Haines, Gail Kay. *The Elements*. New York: Franklin Watts, 1972.

*Irwin, Keith Gordon. *The Romance of Chemistry*. New York: Viking Press, 1959.

*———. *The Romance of Physics*. New York: Charles Scribner's Sons, 1966.

*Kent, Amanda, and Alan Ward. *Introduction to Physics*. Usborne Publishing Ltd., 1983.

Koestler, Arthur. *The Sleepwalkers*. New York: Macmillan, 1968.

Kondo, Herbert. *Adventures in Space and Time: The Story of Relativity*. New York: Holiday House, 1966.

Lapp, Ralph E. *Matter*, Life Science Library. New York: Time-Life Books, 1963.

Ley, Willy. *The Discovery of the Elements*. New York: Delacorte Press, 1968.

*Math, Irwin. *Wires and Watts: Understanding and Using Electricity*. New York: Charles Scribner's Sons, 1981.

*Morgan, Alfred. *A First Electrical Book for Boys*. New York: Charles Scribner's Sons, 1963.

Narlikar, Jayant V. *The Lighter Side of Gravity*. New York: W. H. Freeman, 1982.

Nourse, Alan E. *Universe, Earth, and Atom: The Story of Physics*. New York: Harper & Row, 1969.

*Rosenfeld, Sam. *Science Experiments with Water*. Harvey House, 1965.

*Ruchlis, Hy. *Bathtub Physics*. New York: Harcourt, Brace and World, 1967.

*———. *The Wonder of Light: A Picture Story of How and Why We See*. New York: Harper & Row, 1960.

Sagan, Carl. *Cosmos*. New York: Random House, 1980.

*Silverberg, Robert. *Four Men Who Changed the Universe*. New York: G. P. Putnam's Sons, 1968.

*Sootin, Harry. *Experiments with Electric Current*. New York: W. W. Norton, 1969.

*————. *Experiments with Heat*. New York: W. W. Norton, 1964.

*————. *Experiments with Magnetism*. New York: W. W. Norton, 1968.

*————. *Light Experiments for Home Workshop and School Laboratory*. New York: W. W. Norton, 1963.

Sullivan, Walter. *Black Holes*. New York: Anchor/Doubleday, 1979.

Trefil, James. *From Atoms to Quarks: An Introduction to the Strange World of Particle Physics*. New York: Charles Scribner's Sons, 1980.

————. *Physics as a Liberal Art*. Elmsford, N. Y.: Pergamon Press, 1978.

————. *The Unexpected Vista*. New York: Charles Scribner's Sons, 1983.

*UNESCO. *700 Science Experiments for Everyone*. New York: Doubleday, 1958.

Von Baeyer, Hans C. *Rainbows, Snowflakes and Quarks: Physics and the World Around Us*. New York: McGraw-Hill, 1984.

*Weart, Spencer R. *Light: A Key to the Universe*. New York: Coward-McCann, 1973.

Westphal, Wilhelm H. *Physics Can Be Fun*. Hawthorne Books, 1965.

*Wilson, Mitchell. *Seesaws to Cosmic Rays: A First View of Physics*. New York: Lothrop, Lee and Shepard, 1967.

Wolf, Fred Alan. *Taking the Quantum Leap: The New Physics for Non-Scientists*. New York: Harper & Row, 1981.

INDEX